Muslims' Contribu

Development of

Muhammad Ibrahim H I Surty

Qur'ānic Arabic Foundation

ISBN 1 898596 15 8

Cover and Art Direction by Aftab Ahmed Gharda.
Illustrations by Melanie Tomlinson.

Published by:
QAF: Qur'anic Arabic Foundation,
552B Coventry Road,
Small Heath,
Birmingham B10 OUN,
England,
United Kingdom.

Price: £5.00 + postage

British Library Cataloguing in Publication Data
Surty, Muhammad Ibrahim Hafiz Ismail
Muslims' Contribution to the Development of Hospitals

1. Medicine, Hospital, Islamic Civilization, Education.

ISBN 1 898596 15 8

Printed and bound in Great Britain by
The Cromwell Press Ltd. Melksham, Wiltshire.

بسم الله الرحمن الرحيم

بسم الله الرحمن الرحيم

Dedicated to all staff and patients of the hospitals the world over.

Muslims' Contribution to the Development of Hospitals

Contents

Preface

It is said, Medicine was born; Hippocrates created it. It was dead; Galen revived it. It was scattered; Rhazes (Rāzī) reassembled it. It was imperfect; Avicenna (Ibn Sīnā) perfected it.

Muslim endeavours in the areas of medicine, hospitals and other disciplines clearly manifest the stages stipulated in the above statement. Human civilisation is like a mountain, people come generation after generation, each with their own endeavours, they carve steps on this rocky mountain and facilitate others to ascend.

The most distinctive feature in the all-round development of Islamic civilisation is that it does not ignore, even for a single moment, Allah the Creator of the Universe. One of the principal aims of the Qur'ān and the Sunnah is to grant human beings - the best of Allah's creation - a high position befitting their status and one which enables them to establish their dignity, freedom and honour.

There is a great need to bridge the gulf between the East and the West. Islam can make a positive contribution in bridging the gulf.

It is with these noble aims in mind that this book is presented on the theme of Muslims' contribution to the development of hospitals.

In Section I the Introduction gives an overview of Islam as a Vehicle for Scientific and Intellectual Progress. This context setting effort may assist a Western reader to understand the all-round development Muslims have made in a wide range of disciplines during the Dark Ages, 7th - 13th centuries C.E.

Section II, presents briefly the broad principles of the Qur'ān and the *Sunnah* on Human Dignity, Health, Hygiene and Sickness. This section may aid staff in the hospitals of the West to comprehend Muslim faith and practice.

Muslims' Contribution to the Development of Hospitals

An overview of the Development of Hospitals, their Day to Day Routine and Health Science and Human Dignity is provided in Section III.

Muslims' contribution to hospitals is a vast field and there is a great need for research in a number of aspects related to the subject. It is hoped that this endeavour may inspire others to do extensive researches on this neglected field.

I wish to express my gratitude to Mr Aftab Ahmed Gharda for designing the cover, typesetting and for mounting the hospital sketch and to Mr. Eric R. Fox for his proof reading and valuable suggestions.

Muhammad Ibrahim Surty
Tāj Cottage
Birmingham, England
Ramaḍān 1416 A.H./1996 C.E.

SECTION I

And He (Allah) has subjected to you whatsoever is in the heavens and whatsoever is in the earth; it is all from Him.
Verily! herein surely are signs for a people who reflect.
(The Qur'ān, 45 : 13)

Introduction
Islam as a Vehicle for Scientific and Intellectual Progress (An Overview)

Our aim in presenting a few glimpses of Islam as a vehicle of scientific and intellectual progress is to provide a background to western readers for the scientific and intellectual pursuits of Muslims during the Dark Ages from the7th to 13th centuries C.E.*, enabling them to comprehend the remarkable contributions Muslims have made to the development of hospitals. These contributions are fairly advanced and these achievements are not possible without considerable progress in different disciplines of civilisation. It is essential to present these because many here in the West are completely unaware of Muslims' heritage.

Peoples' achievements for the development of their civilisation can be assessed from their contributions to different spheres of human progress. Muslim contributions to the development of hospitals are numerous. A hospital is an institution which depends heavily on a number of other institutions and industries. A good hospital means that related institutions and industries are flourishing.

The World of Islam Festival, in 1976 in London and a number of distinguished publications covering different disciplines of Muslim civilisation was the first vigorous, systematic and scientific attempt to make the West realise the intellectual and scientific heritage of Muslims and their dynamic contributions in different disciplines of human civilisation, highlighting its principal theme: hierarchy combined with equilibrium.

Unfortunately, this noble project failed during the subsequent years to retain both the enthusiasm and momentum with which it started. Nonetheless, the Festival and its thought provoking literature have left indelible prints in the West and its far reaching effects cannot be ignored. Many scholars have been inspired by this noble endeavour and some have even contributed in different aspects of Islamic civilisation.

---

*Christian Era.

Muslims' Contribution to the Development of Hospitals

Human progress in the field of education and science can be well comprehended through the analogy that a tiny ripple on the surface of still water always helps form large ripples. All civilisations which have emerged in the world inherited the accomplishments of their predecessors and in their own time added their distinctive contribution towards the progress of their own civilisation.

Egypt, Babylon, Assyria, China, India, Greece, Rome, Mexico and Peru are famous for their ancient civilisations. The brilliance of Egyptian civilisation never failed to dazzle scholars the world over. Their remarkable contribution is self-evident in their monumental structures and other relics. These civilisations considerably helped the Greeks to develop their Hellenic civilisation which soon superseded aspects of other civilisations. Hellenic civilisation continued to help in the development of Roman civilisation even after being under its political domination. Socrates, Plato, Euripides and Aristotle were the renowned thinkers and philosophers produced by Hellenic civilisation, whose established code of education and system of philosophy were recognised at all times.

It is very distressing to note that the civilisation that superseded Hellenic civilisation, despite its liberal policy and democratic trends, failed, like all other contemporary as well as older civilisations, to break the shackles of superstition, prejudice, and confinement of education to the privileged class. The rise of Islam saw not only a close relationship between the scientific discoveries and Divine revelation but a positive sacred support extended at all times for their advancement.

'The Muslim empire', says George Sarton, 'was created with the willing collaboration of Greeks, Persians, Copts, Christians, Sabeans and Jews. But this assistance does not wholly explain what might be called *the miracle* of Arabic science, using the word *miracle* as a symbol of our inability to explain achievements which were almost incredible...unparalleled in the history of the world.' [1]

Islam as a Vehicle for Scientific and Intellectual Progress

George Sarton considers Muslim achievements in the arena of science as a miracle. The root cause of this miracle is in fact the unprecedented zeal and spirit the Qur'ān has created for the acquisition of wisdom and knowledge occupying a central position in Muslim scholarship.

In the first place the Qur'ān provides the meaning and significance of the Islamic doctrine and determines its limitless scope.[2] It constantly encourages human beings to use their wisdom and intellect for the conquest of forces of nature for the service of mankind. It also invites the *tadabbur* (contemplation), *tafaqquh* (comprehension), *tafakkur* (thinking), and *ta'aqqul* (wisdom) of men to observe well measured, divinely-guided natural phenomena.[3] It urges human senses and reasoning faculties to investigate first their own bodies[4] and later other things around them.[5] According to the Qur'ān, knowledge and righteousness must go hand in hand.[6] It promises good rewards and high rank for those who possess knowledge coupled with faith and practice.[7]

It is indeed clear from the Qur'ānic principles that the progress of any person lies in the knowledge of created things and careful utilisation of the hidden forces of nature. This is possible only through exploration, observation and experimentation.

Prophet Muḥammad (peace be upon him) propounded the Qur'ānic ideals as much by precept as by his own utterances and actions and became a real pioneer of the modern age. Despite every conceivable torture and cruelty he diverted the course of human thought from unnatural speculation towards concrete reality. With great vigour and courage he cultivated faith, knowledge and action and integrated science with religion. He instructed his zealous Companions to acquire knowledge from any source:

> 'Wisdom is the lost property of a believer where ever
> he finds it he should appropriate it'. [8]

He even set a precedent to acquire knowledge, if possible, even from blood-thirsty enemies.

Muslims' Contribution to the Development of Hospitals

In almost all communities of the past, education was restricted to the ranks of royalty, bureaucracy and priesthood; the common people were not allowed access to knowledge. These communities failed to bring education to the masses. For the first time in human history, the Prophet put into practice the democratic principles of education of the Qur'ān[9] and liberated education permanently from the shackles of class prejudices. He made the acquisition of knowledge incumbent for all and for both sexes.[10] Most early Muslim converts were people from the common strata of the Makkan society including slaves. They received free education from the Prophet. In Madinah the Prophet's students also received free lodging and boarding facilities in the courtyard of his mosque.[11a]

When Muslim Caliphs implemented this new policy of universal, free education in their vast state stretching from the straits of Gibraltar to the gates of India the previously limited number of scholars increased remarkably. The new policy of education provided the common people with an opportunity to decorate themselves with the jewels of knowledge. Very soon scores of common people became first-rate scholars and contributed immensely to different branches of learning.

The Muslim rulers not only granted the facilities of free education to all their subjects but are reported to have pursued knowledge with personal care and great interest. 'Never before and ever since', admits historian Robert Briffault, 'on such a scale has the spectacle been witnessed of the ruling classes throughout the length and breadth of a vast empire given over entirely to a frenzied passion for the acquirement of knowledge. Learning seemed to have become with them the chief business of life. Caliphs and Emirs hurried from their Diwans to closet themselves in their libraries and observatories. They neglected their affairs of the state to attend lectures and converse on mathematical problems with men of science.'[11b]

Islam does not admit the neglect of anything essential for the all-round elevation of humanity: it depends and grows on those truths, beliefs, aims, objects, words and deeds which are concerned with the external and internal training of man who is born to work as a faithful representative of Allah on the earth. The observance of the commandment of Allah and the *Sunnah* of the Prophet is the main springboard of progress in the different spheres of life. Mere spiritual progress at the cost of worldly progress is not recognised in Islam; nor is worldly progress to the exclusion of spiritual upliftment accepted.

Islam considers all intellectual and scientific achievements as the employment of wisdom and development of the faculties invested by Allah in man to recognise His powers through the deep study of His creation. In Islam, art and science are not ends in themselves; they are only means, so far as they do not go against the Qur'ānic principles.

It was a common practice of Muslim intellectuals to begin their treaties with the praise of Allah and salutation to the Prophet. They used to quote on every suitable occasion verses from the Qur'ān as well as *aḥādīth* traditions in support of their arguments. Frequent use of *wallāhu a'lamu*, Allah knows best, at the end of their decision clearly indicates their utmost submission to Allah.

Al-Birūnī, a distinguished Muslim scientist, states in his famous book *Kitāb al-Hind (The Book of India)*:

> 'We ask God to pardon us for every statement of ours which is not true. We ask Him to help us in our endeavours which yield his satisfaction. We ask Him to lead us to a proper insight into the nature of that which is false and idle, that we may sift it so as to distinguishthe chaff from the wheat. All good comes from Him and it is He who is clement towards His slaves. Praise be to God,the Lord of the worlds and His blessings be upon the Prophet Muhammad and his whole family.'[12]

Ibn Sīnā, an outstanding Muslim scientist known in the West as Avicenna, believed that the motions in the heavens and the movements on earth were due to the will of Allah. Life with all its trials and tribulations was devoted entirely to the search for Supreme Truth, which directed the multifarious activities of the universe.[13]

When a Muslim makes a keen observation of the tremendous scientific progress of the modern age, he regards this with the greatest esteem because among other benefits it helps him to comprehend more the Omnipotence of Almighty Allah and the meaning of some of the verses of the Qur'ān. However, when he looks at the moral and social degeneration and penetration of modern scientists and other intellectuals to the darkness of atheism, he becomes sad and worried. He believes that man is the vicegerent of Allah on the earth and he must surrender his being to the Will of the One True Transcendent Allah which promotes him to become an integral part of cosmic harmony and perfect order and grants him tranquillity.

For a better understanding of the remarkable achievements of Muslim scientists and other intellectuals and their attitude towards the pursuit of knowledge, it is not out of place to recall sayings concerning knowledge as mentioned by the Imām Al-Ghazālī in his famous book *Iḥyā 'Ulūm al-Dīn*:

'The basis of happiness in this world and the hereafter is knowledge'.[14]

'Clear understanding and clear intellect are the highest attributes of man, because through the intellect the responsibility of the trust of Allah is accepted and through it man enjoys the neighbourhood of God.'[15]

'Knowledge humbles the haughty youth as the flood washes away the hill.'[16]

'Had it not been for the learned, men would become like animals.'[17]

'Tolerance is the vizier of knowledge, kindness its father, and humility its garment.'[18]

'The best that the learned man can do is either to benefit others by his knowledge or to benefit himself by the knowledge of others.'[19]

'God has not given any of His servants knowledge without giving him tolerance, humility, good nature, and kindness as well.'[20]

Islam as a Vehicle for Scientific and Intellectual Progress

'When the teacher is so fortunate as to possess patience, humility and good nature, the student's lot will be perfected.'[21]

'A teacher should seek no remuneration for his services on behalf of knowledge and accept neither reward nor thanks.'[22]

'As long as a man continues to seek knowledge he remains learned, but the moment he thinks he has mastered all knowledge, he recedes into ignorance.'[23]

'The most wicked among men are the teachers of falsehood.'[24]

'The harm which the unrighteous learned man does is greater than the good.'[25]

Robert Briffault, concludes what has been discussed so far:

> 'For although there is not a single aspect of human growth in which the decisive influence of Islamic culture is not traceable, nowhere is it so clear and momentous as in the genesis of the power which constitutes the paramount distinctive force of the modern world and the supreme source of its victory - natural science and the scientific spirit... What we call science arose in Europe as a result of a new spirit of inquiry; of new methods of investigation, of the method of experiment, observation, measurement, of the development of mathematics in a form unknown to the Greeks. The spirit and those methods were introduced into the European world by the Arabs.'[26]

Acknowledging the outstanding contribution of Muslim scientists, George Sarton states:

> 'The mission of mankind is accomplished by Muslims. The greatest mathematicians Abul Kāmil and Ibrāhīm Ibn Sīnā were Muslims; the greatest geographer and encyclopedist, Al-Masʿūdī was a Muslim; the greatest historian, Al-Ṭabarī was still a Muslim.'[27]

It is sad to observe that the modern world has not fully recognised the immense contribution of Muslims in the field of education and science. John William Draper notes his disapproval of this omission:

> 'I have to deplore the systematic manner in which the literature of Europe has contrived to put out of sight our scientific obligations to the Muhammadans. Surely this cannot be much longer hidden. The Arab has left his intellectual heritage on Europe as, before long, Christendom will have to confess.'[28]

M. N. Roy considers Muslims as the teachers of mankind and the modern world is the inheritor of Muslims renaissance.[29]

A number of factors were responsible for the outstanding achievements of Muslims in different branches of Islamic civilisation, prominent among these were; (a) the rapid territorial expansion, (b) the remarkable progress in Muslim scholarship, (c) the process for the assimilation of a world heritage, and (d)Muslims' contribution to civilisation.

(a) Rapid territorial expansion

A short time after the death of the Prophet considerable territorial expansion had been acquired. The boundaries of the Islamic State stretched from the Straits of Gibraltar to the gates of India. Many renowned cradles of world civilisation were ruled by the Abbasids from the capital city of Baghdad.

The Byzantinian empire was weakened and the Sasanid empire completely defeated. These were the two leading powers of the world which had lived for centuries in hostility. The ʿAbbāsid Caliphate enabled people from these two prominent empires and other ancient cradles of civilisation to interact with each other. It became possible for the citizens of the Islamic State, perhaps for the first time in human history, to move freely from one end of the State to the other in an atmosphere of peace and law and order and to exchange their ideas, thoughts and heritage.

(b) Remarkable progress in Muslim scholarship

The systematic campaign for the codification of the exegesis of the Qur'ān, Islamic sciences and various branches of Arabic language and literature began in the ninth century C.E.. The immense task of codification required a large number of distinguished scholars who were competent and well-versed in Arabic and related disciplines. The field was left open for non-Arabs as well as Arabs to produce celebrated authentic works on a variety of disciplines. The fruits of this scholarship grew and ripened from the seed of universal free education sowed by the Prophet. Those people who learned Arabic for the sake of the Qur'ān, and who were grounded in different branches of learning, successfully accomplished the challenge of codification along with the Arabs and became indisputable authorities on various branches of learning. Arabic which was the *lingua franca* of the multilingual Muslim world played a decisive role in this fruitful exercise. This systematic and painstaking endeavour and dedication produced celebrated treaties in various disciplines. Each witnessed a considerable number of books which were later regarded as master-pieces and sources of related disciplines.

From about the end of the first century *Hijra*, Muslim scholars tended to disassociate themselves from bureaucracy. In general, these scholars refused jobs offered by the government for the sake of their independent services to Islamic disciplines. They tended to adopt vocations that rendered them independent of government support. They chose various forms of labour, but they were unwilling to sacrifice their intellectual integrity by associating with those in authority. They became textile and leather goods manufacturers, jewellers, bookbinders and cobblers,etc. [30]

(c) The process for the assimilation of world heritage

Muslims began their efforts to assimilate the ancient heritage of mankind. For this purpose they established *Buyūt al-Ḥikmah* houses of wisdom. During the reigns of al-Ma'mūn (198/813) and Mu'taṣim (218/833) many books dealing with philosophy, logic, ethics, alchemy, medicine, astrology and mathematics were translated into Arabic. The flexible nature of the Arabic language was invaluable in expressing concrete and abstract ideas.

The Muslim scholars preserved much of the Greek sciences which might otherwise have been lost or remained hidden for many centuries preceding the intellectual awakening in Europe and thereafter the political superiority of the European powers. Furthermore, this liberal and painstaking exercise opened many avenues for Muslims to learn from the past heritages of human civilisation.

(d) Muslims' contribution to civilisation

Soon the process of dissemination began in various other disciplines connected with human progress. Many Muslim scientists, philosophers, historians, geographers, astronomers, physicians, chemists, botanists, linguists etc., appeared on the scene and through life-long study, research, extensive travel, devotion and constant endeavour some of them became universally acknowledged authorities on the knowledge of created things which they then utilised for the service of mankind. They always found in the Qur'ān encouragement and support for their intellectual pursuits. Baron Carra de Vaux writes,

> "The Arabs, thus form a bond of union, a connecting link between ancient culture and modern civilisation. When at the renaissance the spirit of man was once again fitted with the zeal for knowledge and stimulated by the spark of genius, if it was able to set promptly to work, to produce and to invent, it was because the Arabs had preserved and perfected various branches of knowledge, kept the spirit of research alive and eager, and maintained it pliant and ready for future discoveries".[31]

An attempt will now be made to provide a few glimpses of the most outstanding achievements of universally acknowledged Muslim scientists in different branches of science.

The Science of Medicine

Muslim contribution to medical science is immense. They fully recognised the role of physicians in society and therefore awarded them generous emolument and high status.

Muḥammad ibn Zakaria al-Rāzī (Rhazes, 850-923 C. E.) was one of three great physicians. His internationally famous work *al-Ḥāwī (Continents)* published in twenty volumes is a monumental inventory of most of the facts and details connected with medicine. For each disease he provides references to Greek, Iranian, Arabic and Indian authors, and then gives his own opinion. He was a celebrated psychologist. His three works *The Moralities of Perception, Mental Equilibrium and Instinct of Enjoyment* are self explanatory on this branch of knowledge. He very successfully practised and developed psychotherapy, introduced therapeutic methods and invented seton in surgery.

His greatest contribution was his monograph on smallpox and measles, *Kitāb al-Judarī wal Ḥasbah* (*Book on Smallpox and Measles*) was reprinted more than forty times between 1498 and1866 C.E. His *Kitābal-Āsār* became the chief source of chemical knowledge. He was able to transformd Alchemy into Chemistry. His works on stones in the bladder and kidney, his description of the eye, the nose, the ear, and heart are famous.

ʿAlī bin ʿAbbās al-Mujūsī (Hally Abbas) (d.1009 C.E); was a great physician. His two important works *Kāmil al-Ṣināʿah* (*The Perfection of Art*), famous in Latin as *Liber regius* brought him universal fame. He discussed very frankly the merits and shortcomings of the physicians who preceded him.

Abu ʿAlī al-Ḥusain ibn Sīnā (Avicenna, 980-1037), known in the Western world as the "prince of physicians", was the greatest philosopher-scientist of Islam. The materia medica of his *al-Qānūn* (*The Canon*) which contains some seven hundred and sixty drugs is the epitome of Islamic medicine. It provided the main guidance from the 12th to 17th centuries. It is a careful classification and systemization of all the medical knowledge known to the Muslims in the 11th century C.E. The *Canon* distinguishes mediastinitis from pleurisy; recognises the contagious nature of diseases and the spreading of diseases by water and soil. It provides a scientific diagnosis of ankylostomiasis and attributes it to an intestinal worm.

Al-Qānūn is divided into five parts. The first deals with principles of the art of healing, natural matters, causes and symptoms of diseases. It also includes hygiene and laws of therapeutics. The second part contains simple drugs, their properties and uses, in alphabetical order which includes sections on antidotes, cosmetology and fevers. The third part covers discussions on specific diseases from head to toe. The anatomy and physiology of the organs in the body are also provided. The fourth part includes a special discussion on the diseases which are not confined to a particular organ of the body. There is also discussion on cosmetology, fevers, poisons and antidotes. The fifth part deals extensively with compound drugs, serving as a medical formulary of how they are best utilised.

Ibn Sīnā discovered the causes of many diseases such as meningitis, the manner of spread of epidemics, the contagious nature of tuberculosis etc. He foreshadowed the 20th century theory of brain localisation. He believed that the external senses of sight, hearing, tongue, taste and smell were centred in the brain.

His *al-Urjūzah fi al-Ṭib* (Medical Poems), which he composed for medical students in order for them to memorise medical principles on different aspects of medicine, became very popular among medical students.

During the 5th century AH/11th century C.E., ʻArīb ibn Saʻd al-Kātib of Cordova composed a well-known treatise on gynaecology. He was followed by Abul Qāsim al-Zahrāwī (d.1036 C.E.)who was the greatest Muslim figure in surgery.

His book *Kitab al-Taṣrīḥ* (*Concession*) became very popular in the West.Ibn Bayṭār (d.1248 C.E.) in his work *al-Jāmiʿ li-Mufradāt al-Adwiyah wal-Aghdhīyah* (*The Compendium on Simple Drugs and Diets*) based on his own observations and scores of others he has provided in alphabetical order over 1400 simple drugs.

In the curative use of drugs some remarkable advances were made by Muslims. They established the first apothecary shop,, founded the earliest school of pharmacy, produced the first pharmacopoeia and used chemistry for medical purposes. Muslims provided a service for patients with tooth troubles and made artificial teeth from the bones of animals.

Tadhkirat al-Kaḥḥālīn (*The Momento of Ophthalmologist*) by Ali ibn ʿĪsā was an epoch-making treatise on ophthalmology.

Ibn al-Haytham (Alhazen) (d.1039 C.E.) contributed *Kitāb al-Manāzir* (*The Book of Optics*). He pointed out the role of conjuntiva iris, cornea and lens in vision after providing their meticulous description. Ibn Nafīs (d.1413 C.E.) explained the minor circulation of blood while his disciple Ibn al-Quff pointed out clearly the existence of capillaries which were seen three centuries later under the microscope.

Shams al-Dīn Kāshānī was the first physician to contribute an excellent work on first aid. Ibn Zuhar (d.1161 C.E.) was the first physician to recommend the opening of the rectum after failure of the gullet. He was the first parasitologist. His original works, *Al-Taysīr fil-Mudāwāt wal-Tadbīr (Practical Treatments and Precautionary Measures)* supersedes all previous works. Ibn Bajjah (d.1139 C.E.) in his famous work *Kitab al-Nafs* provides a complete survey of peripatetic psychology.

Abū Bakr al-Bayṭār (d.1340 A.C.) was the celebrated veterinary surgeon. His famous work *Kāmil al-Ṣināʿatayn al-Bayṭara wal Zarṭaqa (The Complete Compendium on the Two Arts: Veterinary and Horse Training)* provides comprehensive treatment in both disciplines.

Seyyed Hossein Nasr writes:

> 'In this attempt to view man as a whole,single entity in whom body and soul are united, and in seeking to relate man to the total cosmic environment in which he lives, Islamic medicine has remained faithful to the unifying spirit of Islam. Although originating from the older medical traditions of Greece, Persia and India, Islamic medicine like so many other *Jāhiliyyah* sciences, became profoundly Islamized, and penetrated deeply into the general structure of Islamic civilisation. To this very day, its theories and ideas dominate the daily dietary habits of the Islamic people; they still serve as the framework for a unifying vision of man, as an entity in whom body and soul are closely intertwined, and in whom the state of health is realised through harmony and equilibrium.'[32].

Physics

The contributions of many Muslim scientists can be traced in the field of physics. The most prominent and probably the greatest among them was Ibn al-Haitham (Alhazen) (d. 1039 C.E). In his study of motion he discovered the principles of inertia and thus transformed the study of optics. In refraction he applied the rectangle of velocities at the surface of refraction and also believed in the principles of 'least'. For the first time he drew the eye to detail the phenomenon of expansion of flat surfaces. He discovered the refraction of light in the anatomy of the eye, the formation of pictures on the retina, the enlargement of the pictures, their reflection, accumulation, and the formation of colour.

The *Kitāb Mīzān al-Ḥikmah (The Book of the Balance of Wisdom)* written by Al-Khāzīnī (d.1155 C.E.), is an outstanding contribution to mechanics, hydrostatics and the study of centres of gravity. ʿAbd al-ʿIzz al-Jazarī's *Book of Knowledge of*

Ingenious Geometrical Contrivances is the most interesting treatise on mechanics.

Qayṣar al-Ḥanafī was an expert on the mechanics of the water wheel.

Abū Bakr Rāzī's use of the hydrostatic balance to determine specific gravity marks him out as a brilliant exponent of experimental physics.

Chemistry

Muslim scientists, for the first time introduced three main acids: nitric, sulphuric and hydrochloric. They also discovered the arts of distillation, oxidation and crystallisation by introducing objective and experimental study of the subject.

Jābir ibn Ḥayyān (Gaber, d.815 C.E.) an outstanding Muslim scientist, who was considered to be the father of Muslim Chemistry. His remarkable advancement of the subject both in theory and practice enabled him to explore new methods of evaporation, sublimation, calcination and crystallisation. He was famous for his discoveries of the extraction of sodium carbon, potassium, arsenic and silver nitrates. His famous books are *al-Zibaq al-Sharqī* (*The Oriental Quicksilver*), *Kitāb al-Khāliṣ* (*The Pure Book*), *Kitāb al-Tajammu'* (The Assembly Book), *Kitāb al-Sabi'īn* (*The Seventy Books*) and *Kitāb al-Mīzān* (*The Book of the Balance*). He wrote a large number of works which are known as the Jabirean corpus.

Al-Rāzī classified, for the first time substances into mineral, vegetable and animal. This was regarded as a primary and an all-important categorisation. In the 11th century 'Abd al-Ḥakīm Muḥammad al-Kāshī contributed a book *'Ayn al-Ṣinā'a wa 'Awn al-Ṣuna'a (The Sources for the Art and the Aid to the Students for Alchemy).*

'Modern Chemistry', says Helmot, 'was admittedly the invention of the Muslims, whose achievements in this sphere were of unique interest'.[32]

Mathematics

Muslim mathematicians rescued the useful zero from India and worked on the elaboration of the decimal system, without which the achievements of modern science would have been impossible. They also introduced, on the basis of the Indian digits, Arab numerals which gradually displaced the clumsy Greek symbols and the impossible Roman numerals.

Ghiyāthal-Dīnal-Kāshānī was the greatest Muslim mathematician. He discovered decimal fractions and was the first person to invent a calculating machine and to solve the binomial, known now by the name of Newton.

Logarithms were independently invented by Mullā Muḥammad Bāqī Yazdī.

Nāṣir al-Dīn al-Ṭūsī's treatise *Kitāb Shikl al-Qiṭa'* (*Book of the Figure of the Sector*) revived the science of Trigonometry and was of fundamental importance.

Al-Battānī made mathematical tables of tangents, parallel *nadir* and discovered the law of sines and cosines in Trigonometry.

Algebra

The science of Algebra was invented and introduced by Muslim mathematicians. Algebra is a purely Arabic word, *Aljabr*, which means "a binding together". Muhammad ibn Mūsā al-Khawārizmī (d.850 C.E.) is recognised as the father of Algebra. For five centuries Muslims evolved a more critical and scientific study of equations. Out of several works on this subject by al-Kawārizmī, *Kitāb al-Mukhtaṣar fī Ḥisāb al-Jabr wal Muqābalah* (*The Book of Summary in the Process of Calculation for Compulsion and Equation*) is the most important.

Al-Khawārizmī was undoubtedly one of the greatest and most original mathematicians the world has ever produced. According to George Sarton: "One of the greatest scientists of his race and the greatest of his time".

Geometry

Abul Jūd was the first to solve third-degree equations through geometric solutions. The first work by Muslims on this branch of science is *Kitāb Ma'rifah Misāḥat al-Ashkāl* (*The Book of Knowledge of the Area of Figures*) which stimulated the interest of Muslims in the study of the subject. Abul Jūd devised a geometrical method to divide the circle into nine equal parts. Khayyām and Tusi re-examined the fifth postulate of Euclid concerning the parallel line theorem.

Thābit ibn Qurrah wrote on cubatures and quadrature and used the method of exhaustion in a manner which anticipates the development of integral calculus. He also advanced the study of parabola and in his *Quadrature of the Parabola*, used integral sums to find the area of a segment of a parabola. He introduced the science of calculus and the idea of the centre of gravity. Muslims related geometry to algebra and successfully sought geometric solutions for algebraic problems. They also managed to apply the symbolic aspect of geometry in their art and architecture.

Natural Sciences

Muslims were extremely keen in the study of Natural Sciences. This study included a variety of subjects such as Geography, Geology, Botany, Zoology, Mineralogy, Astronomy, Anthropology, Mythology, Cosmology, etc.

Botany

Muslim scientists in their studies of Botany provided scientific descriptions of various plants which included their classification, physiology, genesis, modes of growth, relation with geographical and climatic conditions and their pharmacological perspective.

Famous works on the subject are Jabir ibn Hayyan's *'Ilm al-Nabāt (The Science of Plants)* and Abū Ḥanīfah Dinwarī's *Kitāb al-Nabāt* which covers physiological, histological and botanical aspects. Ibn al-Sūrī depicted plants in the different stages of their growth.

Zoology

Al-Jāḥiẓ's (d.868 C.E.) famous book *Kitāb al-Ḥayawān (The Book of Animals)* was compiled with principal interest in the existence of Allah and the wisdom of His creation. The book includes the study of three hundred and fifty animals. Al-Fārābī (d.961 C.E.) treated zoology as an independent science. Ibn Sīnā also discussed animal psychology and physiology in his famous book *al-Shifa (Healing)*. Kamāl al-Dīn al-Damīrī (1405 C.E.) combined religious, literary and scientific perspectives in studying animals in his famous book *Ḥayāt al-Ḥaywān al-Kubrā (The Great Book on the Life of Animals)*. It is a zoological encyclopaedia which describes one thousand and sixty-nine animals.

Geography

Muslims contributed immensely in the field of geography. Their outstanding treatise include physical, mathematical, topographical, regional, human, historical, descriptive and specific geography of the known world. Almost all the geographers travelled extensively and mankind benefited greatly from their explorations.

Muslim geographers established correctly the circumference of the earth and measured accurately the length and terrestrial degrees. They devised tables of latitude and longitude of places throughout the world and worked out successfully the means of determining positions.

Muslims were expert navigators. They were familiar with the use of the compass and the astrolabe, an instrument which mapped the position of stars for navigational purpose. They dominated the Indian Ocean and the Mediterranean Sea for five centuries.

The extensive travelling accounts of Ibn Battuta (d.1378 C.E) and Ḥasan Ibn Muḥammad al-Zayyātī were the factors responsible for the exploration of much of the interior of Africa.

Ibn Khurdādhbih was one of the earliest Muslim geographers. His *Kitāb al-Masālik wal Mamālik On Routes and Kingdoms)* was regarded as an outstanding work.

Ya'qubī's (d.857 C.E.) work *Kitāb al-Buldān* (*Book of Countries*) resembles a modern gazetteer. In *Aḥsan al-Taqāsim fi Ma'rifat al-Aqālīm* (*The Best Division for the Knowledge of the Climes*), al-Maqdisī (d.1223 C.E.) divided the land into fourteen divisions. He used symbols in his maps for proper understanding of geographical phenomena. In his maps, routes were coloured red; the golden sand, yellow; the salt seas, green; the well-known rivers, blue; and the principal mountains, drab. considered the earth to be spherical in shape, divided into two equal parts by the equator, and having 360 degrees of circumference, with 90 degrees from the equator to each pole.

Al-Birūnī (d.1048 C.E.) was an outstanding geographer. For the first time he distinguished between a gulf and an estuary. He provided a clear understanding of the phenomena of tides,the increase and decrease in ebb and flow developing periodically parallel with the moon's phases. He provided latitudes and longitudes of numerous places.

Abul Ḥasan al-Mas'ūdī (d.956 C.E.) combined cosmology,, history and geography in his encyclopedic work *Murūj al-Dhahab* (*Prairies of Gold*). Abu Rayḥān al-Birūnī was the master of mathematical, descriptive and cultural geography, and Yaqut's *Mu'jam al-Buldān* (*Dictionary of Lands*) is still an indispensable tool of research for modern scholars. Al-Idrīsī' construction of a celestial sphere and a model of the known world in the form of a disc made him one of the outstanding Muslim cartographers.

Astronomy

Muslims erected well-equipped observatories in almost all big cities of the Muslim world and manifested great skill in the manufacture of the astrolabe.

The study of the science of Astronomy started with actual keen observation of the heavens. Many new stars were discovered and the motion of solar apogee observed. The production of a table for distances of planets and the fixed stars by Farghānī and al-Bīrūnī make them universal astronomers. Muslim astronomers transformed the Ptolemaic spheres from merely models to physical realities. Ibn al-Haytham provided actual physical models for the heavens.

Al-Bīrūnī made a detailed study of solar and lunar eclipses and discovered a new method for determining the time of the appearance of the new moon. Ibn Yūnus solved the problems of spherical trigonometry by means of orthogonal projections.

Al-Farghānī remeasured the diameter of the earth and determined the greatest relative distances and diameters of planets.

Abul Ḥasan invented a telescope from a tube. These were used in the observatories.

Agriculture and Horticulture

Muslims combined intelligently the techniques of Persians, Egyptians, Romans and Byzantines for the promotion of agriculture and horticulture. An excellent network of aqueducts and reservoirs for both domestic and agricultural use was constructed. A large number of wheels were constructed to draw water from wells. Sources of energy such as human, animals, running water and wind were utilised in a number of devices to draw water.

Agriculture was carried on along scientific lines. It was combined with industries. Ahwaz and Fars were famous for sugar cultivation and manufacture. The sugar was supplied to Europe and Asia. When Ferdinand I captured Seville, one of the provinces of Muslim Spain, in 1255 C.E., it possessed several million olive trees and had more than 100,000 mills turning out olive oil.

Spanish Muslims introduced rice, sugar-cane, cotton, ginger, saffron, spinach, flax and sesame and a variety of fruits, vegetables and flowers. All these are borrowed Arabic names in the English language.

The Shapur valley in Persia produced the ten world-famous varieties of perfumed oils extracted from the violet, waterlily, narcissus, palm flower, iris, white lily, myrrh, sweet marjoram, lemon and orange flowers. A variety of roses were cultivated.

A network of canals existed throughout the state. This brought a large tract of land under productive cultivation.

Beautiful gardens were maintained scientifically throughout the Muslim world. These gardens produced several varieties of fruits, vegetables and flowers. *Jannat al-ʿĀrif* (*Generalife*) in Granada, Spain and Shalimar Gardens in Lahore and Kashmir which were developed by Muslims are even today considered among the best gardens in the world.

Numerous scientific works emerged from extensive researches, life-long travels and experience by dedicated Muslim botanists on various plants, their cultivation, growth and natural properties. Mention may be made of a few works:

During the 10th century C.E, Abul Ḥasan al-Qurṭubī contributed the first work on the agricultural calendar, *Kitāb al-Anwār*.

In the 11th century, Abdullāh ibn Bassāl, after extensive travels, contributed his book *Dīwān al-Filāḥa.* This consists of sixteen chapters in which different aspects of agriculture, use of various kinds of water and soil are discussed.

One of the most remarkable contributions is *Kitāb al-Filāḥah* (*Book of Agriculture*) by Ibn al-ʿAwām which provides detailed descriptions of five hundred and eighty-five plants and fifty kinds of fruit trees. It contains striking observations on the different kinds of soil.

The art of incubation was invented in Egypt and introduced to the West later.

Textiles

A variety of beautiful, fabulous and rich fabrics were manufactured by Muslims. Special industries were established for the production of silk. Europeans learned techniques for the production of textiles from Spanish Muslims.

History and Historiography

From the classical period Muslim historians have presented monumental voluminous works. Muslim intellectuals studied other religions and cultures as well.

Ibn Khaldūn (d.1406 C.E.) *Muqaddimah* is an epoch-making work. It covers history, sociology, philosophy, economics and other disciplines. It is an encyclopedic synthesis of the methodological and cultural knowledge necessary to enable the historian to produce a truly scientific work.(EI[2])

Al-I'lān bit Tawbīkh Iimam Zamma Ahl-al-Ta'rīkh (An Open Denunciation of Adverse Critics of the Historians) by al-Sakhawi (d.1497 C.E.) is a monumental work on historiography. He discusses among other important aspects the aims, goals needs for history, blameworthy critics and characteristics of historians.

Islam as a Vehicle for Scientific and Intellectual Progress

The Rise of the University

There was an excellent network of both private and state madrasas, colleges throughout the length and breath of the Islamic State, teaching a wide range of disciplines, competing with each other in providing better free facilities for studies, attracting reputed scholars with handsome emblements in their beautiful buildings by establishing generous pious endowments for this noble cause.

Vigorous and scientific attempts were made by Muslims in the 9th century to found universities. Al-Nizamiyyah was the first university of the medieval and the modern world. Here the lecturers for the first time became civil servants paid by the state. Students received free tuition, lodging and food. Soon Cairo, Fez, Cordova and other leading Muslim cities accommodated their own universities on the same pattern. Al-Azhar University of Cairo is one of the oldest universities in the world. It was founded in the tenth century C.E. and has remained the world's leading Islamic theological centre.

The Universities of Cordova and Toledo in Muslim Spain were not only well known to Europeans but also provided a model for the establishment of European universities.

Arabic: The *Lingua Franca* of Muslims

Arabic, the language of the Glorious Qur'ān, soon became the *lingua franca* of the multilingual Muslim world. It succeeded by means of its proven potentialities in assimilating and incorporating the entire intellectual legacy of the ancient world. This unique language became the medium of all scientific and intellectual Muslim works and played a decisive role in the integration of the Muslim world.

The Qur'ānic text has been and remains the standard of excellence in literary Arabic, and its authority continues to be decisive for many linguistic disputes.

Throughout the course of fourteen centuries this standard of excellence has never permitted any deviation in literary Arabic. As a result of this unique consistency, literary Arabic has been closely associated with the Qur'ānic standard.

The richness of intellectual and scientific contributions can be assessed from the fact that the process of compilation of Arabic manuscripts is not yet complete. Libraries in the Muslim world are busy in this exercise and every day new manuscripts are discovered. Thousands of important works have been lost during the vicissitudes of time. Today, there is a tremendous scope for researchers and scholars in this extremely rich field. Looking at the size of the Muslim contribution it is not an exaggeration to state that the world history of the medieval period will remain incomplete if the historian is either ignorant of or prejudiced against Arabic.

Hamilton Gibb fully realised the importance of the Arabic language. He said:

> 'No one can hope to grasp the human endeavour and the great variety of elements that have entered into the making of Muslim culture, or to comprehend what Muslim culture really is, unless he pursues his quest through the medium of Arabic. The more that other interests obtrude themselves upon the attention of every society, the more necessary it is that some, at least, of those whose task it is to mould the thought and guide the destinies of a Muslim society in the world of today should have a full and clear understanding of its roots. Only so can society maintain that continuity which is as essential for its spiritual life as the succession of generations is for its physical life.'[33]

The link between the East and the West in this modern age is as essential as the air we breathe. In realisation of this great need George Sarton writes:

> "The Arabic culture is a singular intersect to the students of

human traditions in general, to those whose greatest task
it seems to them is the rebuilding of human integrity in
the face of national and international disasters,
because it was... a bridge, the bridge between East and West."[34]

H.R.H The Prince of Wales, recognises fully the contribution of Muslims to civilization and emphasises the need for the West to understand Islam.

"If there is much misunderstanding in the West about the nature of Islam, there is also much ignorance about the debt our own culture and civilization owe to the Islamic world. It is a failure which stems, I think from the straightjacket of history which we have inherited. The medieval Islamic world, from Central Asia to the shores of the Atlantic, was a world where scholars and men of learning flourished. But because we have tended to see Islam as the enemy of the West, as an alien culture, society, and system of belief, we have tended to ignore or erase its great relevance to our own history."[35]

SECTION II

O mankind! Verily! We have created you male and female, and have made you nations and tribes that you may know one another. Verily! The noblest of you, in the sight of Allah, is the best in conduct. Verily! Allah is Knower, Aware.

(The Qur'ān, 49 : 13)

Human Dignity, Health, Hygiene and Sickness
Muslims' Contribution to the Development of Hospitals

The broad principles of the Qur'ān and the *Sunnah* have been regarded and accepted by Muslims as the governing authority in different aspects of human life throughout the generations. It is difficult to ignore their centrality and continuity over the years. Our attempt, therefore, in presenting some broad principles of the Qur'ān and the *Sunnah* for the comprehension of the nature and scope of Human Dignity, Health, Hygiene and Sickness in this section is with the intention of fulfilling two aims: (i) it will narrate Muslims' practice in the past and (ii) their very existence today as an integral part of a Muslim's life will indicate the present day Muslims' faith and practice.

This section may assist the staff of hospitals in the West, as in Europe there are over thirty-five million Muslims and in Britain there are around two million Muslims, most of whom are now citizens of Britain.

Muslims' Contribution to the Development of Hospitals

(a) Human Dignity:

Life is a sacred trust from Allah.[36] It, therefore, must be respected and protected with great care. The Qur'ān affirms that if only one life is saved it is equivalent to saving the lives of the whole of mankind, and if one life is taken unjustly, it is as if the lives of all mankind have been taken.[37]

Allah's pleasure lies in man's fulfilment of His rights and the rights of man's fellow creatures. The Imām al-Bukhārī narrates a *ḥadīth qudsī* [38],- whereby the Messenger of Allah said:

> God, the Lord of Honour and Glory, will say on the Day of Judgement:
> 'Son of Adam, I was sick and you did not visit Me.'
> The man will say: 'My Lord, how could I visit You and You are Lord of the universe!' God will say: 'Did you not know that My servant so and so was sick and you did not visit him? Did you not realise that if you had visited him you would have found Me with him?' [39]

A man's dignity, honour and prestige in the sight of Allah rests in his inner attitude, preparedness, sincerity, devotion and love to fulfil the rights of Allah and the rights of fellow creatures for Allah's pleasure alone.

Those human values which enable a person to accomplish the rights of fellow creatures are presented in the Qur'ān and the *Sunnah* as sound and rich themes. Some of these themes are *al-Taqwā*, Allah consciousness; *al-Ḥaqq*, Truth; *al-Tawakkul*, reliance on Allah; *al-Ṣabr*, patience; *al-Iḥsān*, kindness; *al-Salām*, peace; *al-Shukr*, thanksgiving; *al-'Adl*, justice; *al-Musāwah*, equality; *al-Ukhuwwah*, brotherhood; *al-Ta'āwun*, mutual help; *al-Raḥmah*, mercy; *al-Ḥubb*, love and *al-Maghfirah*, forgiveness. These Qur'ānic themes are extremely rich rich and volumes have been written which elucidate upon them.[40] Over time and in spite of human failings in the past, Muslims have made a significant contribution to civilisation in their understanding of human values.

Human Dignity, Health, Hygiene and Sickness

These are, yet again, very effective age-old prescriptions already tested through millenniums of human experience for human success, prosperity, peace and tranquillity. Divine attributes categorically endorse their link and they are undoubtedly the strong foundations of human dignity.

The Qur'ān respects humans' natural sensorial desire for eternal life. It prescribes a comprehensive life-long programme for training in the temporary worldly life.[41] The trainee returns to Allah and meets in Paradise an eternal abode of peace and tranquillity. This comprehensive training grants a believer further strength to decorate himself/herself with the priceless jewels of human dignity. This exercise even takes note of trivial acts such as smiling at a fellow human being, removing a harmful object from the road and treats both as extremely meaningful and significant exercises.

One of the principal aims of the Qur'ān and the *Sunnah* is to promote man from *al-nafs al-ammārah*, the governing soul, which is the lowest stage to its highest stage of *al-nafs al-muṭma'innah,* the tranquil soul.[42] This ascension grants him the pleasure of Allah,[43] bestows the honour of being the *khalīfah*, vicegerent of Allah on earth[44] and the entire creation is at his service.[45] This promotion clearly means the ascension of a believer on the mountain of humanism because at this lofty position he not only lives, but helps others to live with love, peace, justice and dignity. He becomes a role model for others.

The following are few prominent broad principles from the *Sunnah* of the Prophet for the restoration of human dignity:

No human dead body must be mutilated whether it is Muslim or non-Muslim and whatever the reason for the death.[46]

All human dead bodies must be buried.[47]

Breaking the bones of a dead body shall be regarded as breaking the bones of a living person.[48]

The consumption of human flesh is absolutely prohibited.[49]

Human hair and milk must not be sold as the ones belonging to animals can be sold. However breast-feeding of other peoples' infants for a stipulated period is permitted in case of need, with some returns.[50]

All human beings are descended from Adam and Adam is made of dust,[51] thus no Arab has pre-eminence over a non-Arab and no non-Arab has pre-eminence over an Arab.[52] The criteria for the excellence of one over the other is the level of one's careful observance of Allah's Will.[53]

The Head of the State and the citizens shall remain under the jurisdiction of the *Sharī'ah*, Divine law.[54]

Any citizen enjoys legal rights to file a suit even against the Head of the State.[55]

A person remains innocent unless proven guilty.

The judge shall not discriminate between a Muslim and a non-Muslim, rich or poor, male or female, Arab or non-Arab in the administration of justice. The case shall be adjudicated after a fair trial without any favour and fear.[56]

No citizen, however powerful, privileged and influential he/she may be, has the right to punish fellow citizen/s. The authority and power for the enforcement of *ḥudūd*, legal punishments, shall remain in the hands of the State.

On the theme of *Adab*, Human dignity, Muslims have contributed rich literature covering a wide range of disciplines. Prominent among these are: *Adab al-Qādī, Adab al-Muftī, Adab al-Mu'allimin, Adab al-Kātib, Adab al-Ṭabīb, Adab al-Shahāda, Adab al-Murīd, Adab al-Ṣūfī, Adab al-Faqīr.* Such literature bears testimony that the light of human dignity has not only illuminated the different walks of life of human beings, but has been institutionalised as an important academic discipline.

Human Dignity, Health, Hygiene and Sickness

According to the Qur'ān it is Allah Who grants life and He causes death.[57] From this point begins the journey of the soul to the life Hereafter. Muslims are therefore instructed to say the following Qur'anic prayer whenever they hear of a death:

> Verily! we are Allah's and certainly to Him we are returning.
> (**2** :156)

(b) Health:

Human progress in Islam is divided into three important spheres: the spiritual, mental and physical. Both the Qur'ān and the *Sunnah* provide a well balanced treatment of these aspects and aspire to develop the human personality by presenting a comprehensive course for their attainment.

Faith is the true nourisher of spiritual growth. Knowledge, conviction, sincerity, truthfulness, willingness, submission and profound love are the hard core of faith in Allah which grants a person peace of mind, trust, determination, contentment and other virtues so as to meet a variety of challenges in life. Mental peace plays a decisive role in shaping human behaviour. A believer, therefore, lives and dies for the pleasure of Allah and he/she is afraid of neither life nor death. This sublime mental progress always assists a believer in both health and sickness and does not distract him/her from the path of Allah. It constantly protects him/her against frustration, tension, despair and many other mental problems and keeps his/her vision clear and well guided. It also provides a joy which cannot be described.

Taking proper care of one's health is considered by the Prophet Muḥammad (peace be upon him) to be the right of the body,[58] being one of the great favours which Allah granted man. He further stated: "A healthy believer is better and more lovable to Allah than a weak believer"[59] for an unhealthy person fails to fulfil, owing to his own negligence, the requirements of his body to keep it healthy and strong. It is clear from Qur'ānic principles that, "Allah changes not the conditions of people, until they first change that which is in their hearts."[60]

For, "man has only that for which he strives."[61] And "a person should not forget his share in the world".[62]

A believer is charged to earn his livelihood[63] through lawful means and to take full responsibility for all his dependants.

Food and Drink

The incalculable bounties of Allah[64] have been entrusted to mankind who has been enjoined in the Qur'ān, time and time again, to use this trust judiciously[65] and moderately[66] avoiding excess, waste and squandering.[67] Man is permitted to enjoy an extremely wide variety of food from the herbal, animal and sea worlds for his pleasure and good health. There are however two conditions attached: the food must be *ḥalāl* and *ṭayyib*, good, wholesome and clean. The Qur'ānic dietetic legislations spell out these and they cover both spiritual as well as physical grounds.[68]

Overeating is forbidden by the Prophet. He emphasised that food should be taken only when one feels hungry. One should make sure that one-third of the stomach is filled with food so that there remains a third for water and a third for air.[69] He regarded going to bed on an empty stomach as leading to premature old age[70] and discouraged people from going to bed immediately after taking a meal.[71] It was his habit to go for a walk after supper. The Prophet loved fruits, green vegetables, milk, honey, meat and bread kneaded from unsieved flour.

The Qur'ān prohibits the consumption of intoxicants.[72] The Prophet's campaign in the implementation of this Qur'ānic injunction was not restricted to his generation; its dynamic influence can easily be traced in the life of millions of Muslims across fourteen centuries. By closing the door to intoxicants the health of believers is protected. The Prophet regarded intoxicants as the mother of all evils.[73]

The Prophet forbade drinking in one gulp. Drinking in three breaths one after each sip was regarded by him as more satisfying, healthier and thirst quenching.[74] He forbade drinking directly from a container, rather he advised to pour the liquid into a cup in order to drink it.[75]

Sleep

For good health sound sleep is essential. The best period for such sleep is at night. The Qur'ān says:

> And He it is Who maketh night a covering for you, and sleep repose, and maketh day a resurrection.
> (**25** : 47; see also **78** : 8-11 and **10** : 67)

The prescribed timings for the night and dawn Prayers are such that a person in order to say his dawn Prayer before sunrise is required to go to bed after night Prayer which is usually said after supper. The timings of both Prayers regulate sleep.

Sexual Life

Sexual desires are natural human desires and their relationship with health cannot be over-emphasised. A person is permitted to fulfil sexual desires through the institution of marriage only.

The *Sharī'ah,* Islamic Law for the matrimonial relationship constructs in Qur'ānic terms a fortified castle of justice, peace, chastity, piety, mutual love, mercy and affection between the two spouses.[76] The Qur'ān strictly forbids sex outside marriage and leaves no room for sexual promiscuity and homosexual relations. The Qur'ān even prohibits sexual intercourse with one's wife during her menstrual period.[77]

The strict Qur'ānic legislations protect a Muslim's health from various diseases such as venereal diseases, cancers, infections, inflammations, acquired immune deficiency syndrome (AIDS), to mention but a few.

Exercise

The exercises necessary for good health are elaborated on in the authentic *Sunnah* of the Prophet and are established by a number of *ahadith,* traditions.

The Prophet believed that if health and leisure hours are not properly utilised people can be deceived.[78]

(c) Hygiene:

The Qur'ān not only insists on bodily cleanliness and clothing,[79] but also enjoins people to adorn[80] these moderately[81] and condemns those who regard adornment as unlawful.[82] The Prophet said: "Verily Allah is beautiful and loves beauty."[83] The practical teachings of the Prophet on hygiene included many aspects, prominent among these were the human body, health, clothing, sex, diseases, the healing properties of certain foods and the preventative measures to be taken against epidemic diseases and pollution. The following Prophetic *Sunnah* and traditions can be cited, in this respect:

Ritual purity and cleanliness are integral parts of Faith and both are related to the human soul and body respectively.

The use of perfume grants delight to the human mind and soul. The Prophet loved wearing it.[84]

The use of clean water is required for ritual purity and any other cleaning. The water must be free from odour, colour and taste.

In *wuḍū̄*, ablution, which is obligatory for ritual Prayer,[85] thrice with clean running water: the mouth cavity and nostrils are rinsed, hands are washed along with the elbows and feet including the ankles; and the head is lightly rubbed once with a wet hand. Water soiled through body immersion is regarded as unclean. This means that after taking a bath in a bath tub the body must be washed thrice, with clean running water. After serving the calls of nature the polluted parts may either be soaked or preferably thoroughly washed thrice, with clean running water so that the odour disappears.[86] The hands must be washed thoroughly afterwards.

Clothes and other objects polluted with urine, stool, blood and other unclean substances must be washed thrice with running water.

The taking of a bath *ghusl* becomes obligatory[87] after ejaculation of semen or sexual intercourse, menstruation and after the post natal bleeding period.

Sick persons who are unable to use water either for *wuḍū* or *ghusl* are exempted. They can do *tayammum*, dry ablution.

Cleaning the teeth with a tooth brush, *siwak,* is highly recommended before each of the five obligatory Prayers.

Breast feeding is highly recommended.

Removing hair growth from the armpits and under the navel once a month, keeping facial hair tidy, circumcision and clipping the nails are emphasised.[88]

The Prophet forbade urinating into a pond or reservoir and relieving oneself in the shade of a tree.[89] He instructed to keep courtyards and surroundings clean.[90]

Concerning contagious diseases and epidemics, the Prophet instructed:

(a) 'Do not bring sick (camels) along with healthy ones to a watering place.'[91]

(b) 'When you come to know the spread of plague in a land you should not visit that place. But if it has already spread in a land in which you are present then you should not desert the place.'[92]

(c) 'In order to protect oneself from droplet infection it is always better to speak to, for instance, a leper by keeping a certain distance.'[93]

Hygiene was never out of sight of the Prophet throughout his life. He vigorously implemented the Qur'ānic principles on hygiene and demonstrated this clearly in his day to day, public as well as private life. He taught hygiene to his zealous and dedicated Companions. *Al-Ṭahārah*, ritual cleanliness, was transformed into a religious law and was regarded by the Prophet as an integral part of faith. Throughout the period of Islam all celebrated treatises on Islamic law included a chapter on *al-Ṭahārah* and independent treatises have been contributed on this theme as an integral part of faith.

(d) Sickness:

Allah is the Healer[94] and the Qur'ān exhorts that a believer in sickness should turn to Him because sickness is a trial which demands faith, patience, courage, determination and hope.[95] This trial the Prophet stated is an expiation *kaffārah,* of sins:

> A believer does not suffer from any sickness, continuous pain,
> anxiety, grief or injury or a thorn which pricks his skin
> without forgiving him his wrong actions on account of this.[96]

This attitude of mind enables the sick to face sickness with patience, determination, courage, hope and trust in Allah. It helps to clear the dark clouds of distress, frustration, fear and pessimism. Generally it has been observed that in sickness believers do turn more towards Allah in supplications and even thank Him. The Prophet stated that sincere supplication of the sick are accepted. Perhaps this is the reason why visitors when they make supplication for the recovery of the sick, request the sick to pray for them.

The Prophet not only instructed sick people to take medicine but he himself invited expert physicians for this purpose.[97] For medicine and cure he made the following thought provoking statement:

Human Dignity, Health, Hygiene and Sickness

Allah has not created any disease without also creating
a medicine or a remedy for it.[98]

It clearly means that for all diseases if a remedy is not found researchers should not give up their researches to discover the cure. It closes the doors of pessimism in the research and boosts the morale of the researchers.

The Prophet made a quack responsible for the consequences of his/her practice.[99] This clearly indicates that sickness should be cured with knowledge. Expert physicians and *'ulamā'* were regarded by the Prophet as indispensible people.[100] He himself used to take medicine and even suggested the use of certain food as a cure for certain ailments. Special treatises have been contributed by Muslims on the theme of the Prophet's practice of medicine and this discipline is known as *Ṭibb al-Nabī*[101] and has remained very popular among Muslims throughout the generations.

The Prophet prevented people from forcing a patient to eat if he refuses to eat but if he has an appetite for something, the Prophet advised to feed him.

Ailing people always received the most tender and kind treatment from the Prophet.[102] A visit to a sick brother was regarded by the Prophet as the right of a believer.[103] The visitor gains the mercy[104] and pleasure of Allah and walks along the high road to Paradise.[105] He recommended that sympathy and prayer be offered for the recovery of the sick.[106] The visitor is advised by the Prophet to place his hand on the forehead of the patient and say: "All well and good, may this be a means of purification, *inshāAllāh*."[107]

One of the Prophet's favourite *du'ā'* supplications was:

O Allah, take away this illness. O *(Rabb)* Lord of mankind,
heal this for You are the Healer. There is no cure,
except from You - a cure which leaves no illness behind.[108]

The visitor should not prolong unnecessarily the duration of his visit more than the time it takes to twice milk a she-camel.[109] He should neither suggest a remedy to the patient nor scare him.

The Prophet in his visits did not discriminate against ailing people, he even visited sick non-Muslims.[110] According to one of the Prophet's statements, compassion must be shown to all on earth in order to win Divine Compassion. This practice of the Prophet clearly illustrates that this is a human duty which cuts across the barriers of race, religion, colour and nationality.

SECTION III

Whoever kills a human being, not in lieu of another human being nor because of mischief on earth, it is as if he has killed all mankind: And if he saves a human life, it is as if he has saved the lives of all mankind.
(The Qur'ān, 5 : 35)

The Development of Hospitals in the Muslim World
Muslims' Contribution to the Development of Hospitals

Unfortunately not much research has been carried out on the institution of the hospital and its development in the Muslim world. Ahmad 'Isa Bak's *Ta'rīkh al-Bīmaristānāt fil Islām (History of Hospitals in Islam)* in Arabic published in 1939, appears to be the first book available on the subject. The attempt though good it is not comprehensive. It is true that very scanty material is available in the sources, nonetheless, the need for extensive research in this vast area is long overdue.

In this short work an attempt is made to provide an overview of a few of the most distinguished hospitals in the Muslim world, based on the available data. This data, itself is limited in the sense that it does not include the development of hospitals in many prominent regions of the Muslim world, such as Muslim Spain, Turkey, Iran and other regions. The field of research is vast and needs not one, but several projects to do justice to the subject. Our aim in this work is to stimulate the interest of researchers to undertake extensive researches on the related aspects of this neglected and unexplored field.

Muslims' Contribution to the Development of Hospitals

The establishment and development of hospitals is not possible without two extremely important factors: economic prosperity and the zeal from philanthropists for public welfare. In Islam *al-Zakah* (welfare due), has been made obligatory, developed as its religious law and regarded as a clear sign of faith. The emphasis placed on charity in the Qur'ān is such that a true believer cannot remain heedless of this noble exercise.

Besides the second pillar of Islam *al-Zakah* (obligatory charity) and *Sadaqah* (voluntary charity), another charitable institution *waqf* (pious endowment), was introduced by the Prophet. The word *waqf* in Arabic literally means 'stopping', 'binding', 'keeping in custody' or 'detaining'.[111] In Islamic Law *waqf* denotes the extinguishment of the proprietor's ownership in the property dedicated and its detention in the implied ownership of Allah in a manner that its usufructs may accrue to or be applied for the benefit of humanity.[112]

The institution of *waqf* has remained extremely popular among Muslims throughout the generations. One can understand its importance from the fact that at the beginning of the nineteenth century C.E., 75% of arable land, estimated value 50,000, 000 Turkish pounds, was endowed as *waqf*. By the end of the nineteenth century C.E., 50%, 33% and 12.5% repectively of cultivable land in Algiers, Tunis and Egypt was dedicated as *waqf*, pious endowment.[113]

Islamic Law provides another opportunity to Muslims for public welfare, by allowing a Muslim to bequeath one-third of his/her property. These inner Muslim attitudes and practice, which undoubtedly constitute a paramount requirement of faith for the elevation of human dignity and honour, have enabled both the rich and poor members of the Muslim society to promote vigorously vigorously the institution of hospitals in the Muslim world. There is no doubt that the State played a decisive role in the establishment of the network of hospitals in the Muslim world, but there is ample evidence that philanthropists from their wealth and the poor from their labour and goodwill contributed immensely to this noble cause.

The Development of Hospitals in the Muslim World

The Foundation

The Prophet's mosque in the capital city of Madinah served many practical purposes and acted as a nucleus for a number of Islamic institutions which are essential for public welfare. This great centre accommodated the first Muslim hospital service in its courtyard. In the battle of the Ditch when the Prophet came across some wounded soldiers he ordered that a special tent be erected in the courtyard of the mosque and these soldiers be accommodated in the tent for medical aid. A lady nurse was also attached to the tent to look after these soldiers.[114]

The Imām al-Bukhārī (d.870 C.E.), has included the above mentioned report in his *al-Jāmi' al-Ṣaḥīḥ*, which is regarded as an authentic source. The analysis of the report may assist us to comprehend the importance of the institution of the hospitals for the Muslim society.

(i) As it is mentioned in Section II, that the Prophet regarded two people as indipensable -*'ulamā,'* scholars and *aṭibbā'*, physicians - for a society. It clearly shows that both these institutions which they represent are extremely important for a society. The Prophet's order to set up a tent for service as a hospital in the courtyard of his mosque was a very significant step. The Prophetic Mosque, for Muslims of all ages and regions is a sacred place which is highly venerated. venerated. Pilgrims in their thousands visit the Mosque from different parts of the world. The site for the tent could have been selected anywhere in Madinah. The very existence of the tent (a temporary hospital) in the courtyard of the Prophetic Mosque and a few yards from the residence of the Prophet, clearly indicates that the institution is extremely important for the restoration of Human dignity. Through this *Sunnah*, a precedent is set by the Prophet for Muslims of all ages that they should not ignore the desperate need of this great institution.

(ii) The patients of this tent (hospital) thus realised that the Head of the State and other members of the society were most willing to extend their care, sympathy and prayer for their recovery.

(iii) This practical wisdom made the citizens of the capital city of Madinah conscious that the patients needed their attention, care and prayers.

(iv) The appointment of a woman nurse clearly suggests that women by their nature are suitable to render the services needed by the patients.

(v) The immense contributions which Muslims have made for the development of hospitals stand as beautiful edifices on the foundation laid by the Prophet.

During the early Islamic period, attempts were made by the Muslims to provide appropriate facilities and assistance to sick people.

The ten years (13/634-23/644) under the rule of the second Caliph 'Umar ibn al-Khaṭṭāb saw many public welfare works in the Islamic State. The Caliph was so concerned for the welfare of ailing people, that he accompanied a team of physicians with the army proceeding towards Persia.

During the Umayyad period (86/705-96/715), Walīd ibn 'Abd al-Malik founded a hospital for the blind, lepers and other disabled people. He himself laid the foundation stone. In his hospital lepers were not permitted to mix with other people.[115] He took the lead in establishing a dispensary which was well equipped in respect of both physicians, surgeons and drugs. This dispensary served as a model and on its pattern several dispensaries were established in the Muslim world during the Umayyad period.

Muslim jurists of both the early and the late Islamic period always tried to postulate in a systematic and comprehensive manner, the legal opinions for the application of Islamic laws concerning medicine. This has always served as a guideline to Muslim physicians in their practise of medicine and surgery.

Old Hospital

Caliph al-Manṣūr (136-158/754-575), regarded as the founder of the round city of Baghdad, constructed a *Bīmāristān*, hospital in an old suburb of great importance known as Karkh which was situated south-west of the original walled city. The city was beautiful having in front of it the great Karkhaya canal, a branch of the Isa Canal, which joined the waters of the Euphrates to those of the Tigris. An arched stone bridge over the canal was known as the *Qanṭrarah al-Bīmāristān*, Hospital Bridge.

The hospital proved to be the cradle of the Baghdad school of medicine. Here physicians from the time of Bakhtīshū to Rāzī lived, lectured and practised. It was later known as the 'Old Hospital' until the appearance of the 'Adudi hospital in the tenth century. This hospital served as the chief centre of clinical teaching and practise.[116]

Rashidi Hospital

'Abbāsid Caliph Hārūn al-Rashīd (170/780-193/809) established a hospital in Baghdad in 190/805 and provided the necessary facilities for this hospital. He recruited the chief physician of the famous medical centre of Persia, Jundishāpūr, Jibrail ibn Bakhtīshū who was appointed as the provost of the Baghdad hospital. Other physicians of Jundishāpūr were also attracted towards Baghdad and soon the reputation of Jundishāpūr diminished. The hospital at Baghdad became a centre for medical activities in the Muslim world. Five more hospitals were established on its pattern.[117] So much so that the minister of the Caliph Hārūn al-Rashīd, Yaḥyā ibn Khālid Barmakī constructed a hospital on the pattern of the Rāshidī hospital in Baghdad with his own funds.[118]

Caliph Hārūn al-Rashīd also established a separate Department of Health. Several government dispensaries were established under this department. Ibn

Bakhtīshū was the first to be appointed as Inspector General. His son Jibrail also held the same post. They earned handsome salaries from the state and were respected in the society. Attempts were made to raise their standards of living considerably.

Bimaristan al-Sayyidah

In *Muḥarram* 306/918, Caliph Muqtadir's court physician Sinān bin Thābit, persuaded the Caliph to construct a hospital in the famous market of Sūq Yaḥyā on the bank of the river Tigris, which was known as *Bīmāristān al-Sayyidah*. Six hundred dinars monthly were spent on this hospital.[119]

The Caliph's mother left a pious endowment for the hospital *al-Badrī*. Once when its director Abū al-Saqr failed to send the funds, Sinān bin Thābir complained to 'Alī ibn'Īsā the finance minister. 'Alī ibn'Īsā informed him that due to the winter weather, patients were experiencing hardship without coal and woollen garments. Abū al-Saqr was asked to explain.[120] This reflects the concern for the welfare of the patients in the hospital. Every attempt was made to provide the patient's necessary facilities.

In 319/931 physicians made some mistakes in their treatment of a patient as a result of which the patient died. Immediately the Caliph ordered Sinān ibn Thābit who was the Inspector General of Health of the Islamic State, to examine the proficiency of all physicians. Arrangements were made for practical instruction. Opthalmologists were examined to ascertain whether they were acquainted with anatomy in order to carry out surgery. They were forbidden to practice unless they knew the anatomy of the eye-ball. Physicians were not allowed officially to start practising before obtaining a proficiency diploma. Sinan granted diplomas to eight hundred and sixty physicians in Baghdad.[121] This in itself clearly manifests the concern for life and the popularity of the practice of medicine in the city of Baghdad alone. This practice is common in this modern age, especially in developed countries.

The Development of Hospitals in the Muslim World

Muqtadiri Hospital

In 303/716 Caliph al-Muqtadir (295-319/908-932) asked the famous physician Abu 'Uthmān Sa'īd bin Ya'qūb from Damascus to supervise the hospitals in Baghdad, Makkah and Madinah. Caliph Muqtadir also commissioned several new hospitals to which he endowed large funds. Of these the Muqtadiri hospital was the most famous. He had a talented minister 'Alī ibn 'Īsā al-Jarrāḥ who was famous for his extraordinary administrative skills and had a keen interest in the welfare of the common people. This minister wrote to Sinan, the Inspector-General of Health, in respect of the affairs of prisoners:

> I thought over the affairs of the prisoners. The prisons include large number of prisoners and their abode is against the will of prisoners, which may become a factor responsible for the spread of disease. You should send physicians to examine the prisoners every day. They should go round all the prisons and treat those prisoners that are ailing.[122]

It was probably because of his instructions that physicians thereafter made daily visits to jails.

The same minister is reported to have instructed the Inspector General of Health with regard to rural health care:

> I thought over the treatment of those people who are residing in rural areas. Since the villages are remote places from the clinics of practising physians and that there must be ailing villagers residing in these villages, you should therefore send teams of physicians together withmedicines and drugs to go round the villages. They shouldhalt at every locality for a period which its inhabitants woulddemand of them. They should treat such cases and should move on afterwards to other places. [123]

This practice continued in the Muslim world so much so during the time of Sultān Maḥmūd al-Seljūqī (485/1092) the number of physician teams amounted to forty. Sinān was also responsible for the establishment of dispensaries for animals.

The provision of public health facilities into rural areas by the State was probably the first of its kind in the world. It was a mammoth task which needed huge resources and many well- qualified staff. Its implementation indicates the concern the State had for public health and draws attention to the existence of a large number of qualified physicians. Furthermore, their concentration in the rural public health programme shows that the urban population were enjoying the services offered by a large number of well established hospitals.

The radius for the construction of hospitals began to rapidly enlarge. It included principal cities like Makkah, Madinah, Shiraz, Ray, Nisapur and so on.

Muqtadir's minister 'Alī ibn'Īsā constructed a hospital, Bīmāristān Ḥarbiyyah in a quarter of Baghdad known as Ḥarbiyyah. He spent an enormous amount of money on its construction.[124]

The minister Ibn al-Furāt constructed a hospital in Baghdad named after him Bimaristān Ibn al-Furāt. He appointed Sinān ibn Thābit's son in charge of it.[125]

Ibn Ṭūlūn Hospital in Egypt

Ibn Ṭūlūn, Governor of Cairo in 259/872, established a hospital on the pattern of the leading hospital at Baghdad.[126] He spent 60,000 dinars on this project alone. He set aside a handsome endowment fund for the maintenance of the hospital and the welfare of the sick people without discrimination.[127] This enabled the management of the hospital to provide free accommodation, treatment and food to patients. Admitted patients were granted a special hospital apparel. Attempts were also made to provide excellent medical care by recruiting renowned physicians who examined the patients twice daily. The hospital was well equipped with all available medical facilities and drugs.

This hospital was divided into two main sections: male and female. These were further divided into a number of halls. These large halls were divided into small rooms to accommodate patients suffering from different diseases so that full attention could be given to their care. In addition, various separate wards were constructed for eye diseases, orthopedic and surgical cases. There were two principal sections of the hospital; an outpatient and an in-patient section. Ibn Tulun took a personal interest in the welfare of the hospital. It was his habit to visit the hospital every Friday to inspect the progress of the patients. A separate section of the hospital building was used for the treatment of the insane.[128]

This hospital had a huge library containing around one hundred thousand volumes. As these volumes were kept in the hospital, most were likely to be in the field of medicine and the health sciences. This reflects the enthusiasm and scholarship in these fields.[129]

ʿAḍuḍī Hospital in Baghdad

The largest hospital in the Muslim world, which could also be regarded as a celebrated medical University was the ʿAḍuḍī Hospital in Baghdad. The supremacy of this hospital was recognised for at least four centuries in the Muslim world. It provided the best available medical facilities. This important hospital was founded by ʿAḍuḍ al-Dawlah in 368/978 and was endowed with 100,000 dinars.[130] It flourished up to 656/1258 but was then devastated by the Mongols when they invaded Baghdad.[131]

Sūq al-Māristān, a small quarter is situated between Bāb al-Basrah and Shāriʿ Ām. It was in this quarter that this hospital was situated. Its beautiful and magnificent building was constructed on the banks of the river Tigris. It contained many rooms. The hospital building was divided into wards and each ward was like a Royal quarter. The hospital was equipped with up-to-date treatment facilities. The patients were treated kindly. All patients received medicine and food free of charge. On every Monday and Thursday the leading physicians of the city visited this hospital and provided a consultancy service to the hospital's physicians.

A large number of auxiliary staff were recruited for cooking food and the preparation of medicine. Some of them also served food and the medicine to the patients according to the prescription of the physicians.[132] A record of the ailment and cure was kept.

Many medical specialists were recruited to serve in this hospital from different parts of the Muslim world. Ibn Baksh, Abū 'Īsā and Ya'qūb were among the renowned physicians who not only practised medicine, but also delivered lectures and provided the necessary training to medical students.
Elgood writes:

> All these [hospitals] were overshadowed by the hospital that he ['Aḍuḍ al-Dawlah] founded in Baghdad, complete with equipment, numerous trust funds and a pharmacy stocked in drugs brought from the ends of the earth."[133]

In 449/1057 'Aḍuḍī Hospital was renovated by Caliph al-Qā'im bi Amrillāh. He increased the number of beds in the hospital and provided all the necessary facilities for both staff and patients. It is indeed fascinating to note that an expensive commodity like ice was made available for patients.[134] A beautiful garden was established by the side of the hospital and included a variety of fruit trees and herbs. Boats would transport, along the canals in the hospital grounds patients who were unable to walk from one section of the hospital to another. Physicians were on duty day and night and slept on the premises in order to attend to emergency cases immediately.

Bīmāristān al-Kabīr in Damascus

In Damascus, Nurūddin Zinkī (51-569/1118-1174) established a magnificent hospital. It was famous both as Nūriyyah and Bīmāristān al-Kabīr Damishq. It soon became famous in the Muslim world because of its excellent service and the personal attention paid to it by the ruler. Every facility and comfort which the regime could afford was provided for the patients. Reputed physicians and surgeons such as Mahadhdhab al-Dīn bin al-Naqqāsh (d. 573/1178), Shamsh al-Dīn, Kamāl al-Dīn Ḥimṣī, 'Imād al-Dīn, Rashīd al-Dīn bin Khalīfah, Jamāl al-Dīn al- Raḥbī and Abū al-Majd were invited to serve at the hospital, thus adding considerably to its fame.[135]

Its beautiful wooden doors were prepared by the famous carpenter Mu'īd al-Dīn.[136] Many auxiliary staff including scribes were also recruited. The scribes maintained a register of the patients which also recorded the expenses incurred on each one. Both rich and poor were treated free in this hospital. The comforts and the facilities enjoyed by the patients can be assessed in a facinating report by Ṭāhirī:

> When I was travelling in 831/1427, I entered Damascus hospital after observing a wide variety of food and drink being served to the patients. I pretended to be a patient and registered my name in the register of the hospital. The chief physician of the hospital examined me and prescribed delicious food, meat, chicken, sweets and excellent fruits. The physician however, in view of his sharp wit and experience, diagnosed thereal disease. He therefore, after three days sent a letter orderingthat the guest was not permitted to stay for more than three days.[137]

Ibn Jubayr reported that in this hospital a register of patients was kept. It was the practice of the physicians to record, after a routine daily examination of each patient, his/her diet and medication requirements.[138]

Nūr al-Dīn donated a large number of medical books. These were placed in a large hall that served the dual purpose of a library and a lecture theatre.[139]

Muslims' Contribution to the Development of Hospitals

Dimnah Hospital in Qayrawan

The Aghlabiyyah Prince Ziyat Allāh (201-223/817-838) built the first Dimnah hospital in Qayrawan in North Africa. The halls were well organised indicating waiting rooms for the visitors and a mosque for the prayers and religious teaching. Sudanese women were employed as nurses. *Dār al-Judhāmah*, the house of the lepers, was also constructed near the hospital.[140]

Hospital in Morocco

Al-Manṣūr Ya'qūb bin Yūsuf (579-595/1184-1199), the Muwahhid ruler, built a hospital in Morocco in 586/1191. The historian ʿAbd al-Wāḥid al-Marrakushī has provided the following account, when he witnessed the construction of the hospital:

> Here was constructed a hospital, which I think is unequalled in the world. First, a large open space in the most level part of the town was selected. Orders were then given to architects to construct as fine a hospital as possible. So the workmen embellished it with beautiful sculptures and ornamentation even beyond what was demanded of them. All manner of suitable trees and fruit trees were planted there, and water was made to flow in abundance, flowing through all the rooms. In addition, there were four large pools in the centre of the building, one of which was lined with white marble. The hospital was furnished with valuable carpets of wool, cotton, silk and leather, so wonderful that I cannot even describe them.
>
> A daily allowance of thirty dinars was assigned for all necessary foodstuffs, exclusive of the drugs and chemicals which were on hand for the preparation of draughts, unguent, and collyria. Day-dresses and night-dresses, thick for winter, thin for summer, were provided for the use of patients.

After he was cured a poor patient would receive on leaving the hospital a sum of money sufficient to keep him for a time. Wealthy patients had their money and clothes returned to them. In short, the founder did not confine the use of the hospital to the poor or to the rich. On the contrary, every stranger who fell ill at Marrakesh, was carried there and treated until he either recovered or died. Every Friday after the mid-day Prayer, the prince mounted his horse to go and visit the patients. He used to ask how they were and how they were being treated.[141]

Bīmāristān al-Ṣaliḥānī Ayyūbī

The Sultān Ṣalāḥ al-Dīn Ayyūbī converted a palace in Cairo into a hospital in 577/1181.[142] On its wall the entire Qur'ān was written. Ibn Jubayr describes this hospital in these words:

> This hospital is one of the prides of Ṣalāḥ al-Dīn. This is a magnificent and beautiful palace. The rooms are most elegant. In each room beds are spread on which mattresses and pillows are placed in an orderly manner. There is a separate room for the dispensing of medicine and for this purpose chemists and compounders have been appointed. For lunatics there are separate houses which include a vast courtyard.
>
> The management of the hospital is in the hands of a physician under whom many auxiliary staff are working. They examine the patients day and night and they change a patients medication and diet making modification (for the comfort and recovery of patients). The Sultān himself always visits the hospital and keeps himself informed about the treatment and comfort of the patients.[143]

Sultān Ṣalāh al-Dīn also constructed a hospital in Alexandria. A special feature of this hospital was that those patients who for some reason preferred to remain at home could do so. They received their treatment from a team of physicians and surgeons who were asked to visit them and treat them in their homes.[144]

Rulers' interest in the construction of hospitals started to increase from this period. Muslim rulers of different dynasties began competing with each other both in the size of the hospitals they constructed and the facilities they provided for patients. The result of this competition was excellent. Each celebrated city of the Muslim world accommodated more than forty hospitals.

This fact is attested to by an historian named Benjamin of Tudela, a Jew who visited Baghdad in 556/1160. He found at least sixty medical institutions there and wrote:

> All are well provided for from the king's stores with spices and other necessaries. Every patient who claims assistance is fed at the king'sexpense until his cure is complete. There is another large buildingcalled Darul Maraphtan in which are locked up all thos insanepersons who are met with during the hot season, everyone of whomis secured by iron chains until his reason returns when he is allowed to return home. They are regularly examined once a month by theking's officers appointed for this purpose and when they are found to be possessed of their reason again, they are immediately liberated. All this is done by the king in pure charity towards all those who come to Baghdad either ill or insane, for the king is a pious man and his intention is excellent in this respect.[145]

Al-Manṣūrī Hospital:

This hospital was commissioned by Malik al-Manṣūr Sayf al-Dīn Qalāwun immediately after his ascent to the throne in Cairo in 683/1284. The king made a vow when he was cured by medicine supplied from the Nūriyyah hospital in Damascus that he would commission a hospital if Allah would make him king.[146]

The hospital was developed in a palace which was extended, occupying an area of ten thousand square metres. Its pillars were made of marble. It took eleven months to complete. The king was so interested in the project that he inspected the site every day. The building was regarded as one of the finest buildings in Cairo.

Its ruins still exist in Shāri‘ Taḥsīn.[147] Water was supplied to the hospital through a special canal. By a public proclamation, the king made the services of the hospital available to all, male, female, natives and foreigners, known and unknown, slaves and free people.[148] Provision was even made for patients who had not registered in the hospital so that they could benefit from its medicine. The hospital donated new clothes to each cured and discharged patient and took full responsibility for the funeral services of those patients who passed away.[149]

The hospital was divided into a number of wards for different diseases. Male and female patients were kept in separate wards. For teaching, administration, the preparation of medicines, kitchen and storage there were separate buildings. All these places were connected with a canal to ensure a constant supply of water.[150]

Every day hundreds of people visited the hospital and a large quantity of medicine was supplied to patients. It is reported that five hundred pounds of pomegranate syrup alone was consumed every day.[151]

Because of its excellent service, al-Mansuri Hospital became so advanced that it can safely be placed at the same level as a modern, well organised hospital. The most outstanding characteristic of this hospital was that, like the advanced hospitals in the modern world, provisions were made to entertain patients with light music. Professional story tellers were appointed to narrate stories and jokes to the patients. *Mu'adhdhinūn* sang religious songs in their melodious voices before the morning *'adhān* (call for Prayer) so that suffering patients might forget their suffering.[152] It is fascinating to note that this hospital is rendering its services even to the present time.[153]

Hospitals in the Muslim world were of two kinds, established and mobile. As stated earlier, the vice-minister 'Īsā bin'Alī al-Jarrāḥ, instructed Sinān the Inspector-General of Health, to begin mobile clinical services for villagers in the rural areas. Teams of physicians visited far-flung villages to attend to their ailing inhabitants.

S.K. Hamarneh writes:

> Hospitals in Islam generally were under trained administrative authorities, physicians, surgeons and pharmacists associated with the hospitals, as well as those in management and labour, were all from the laity. Even more remarkable is the fact that Christian physicians who belonged to the Eastern churches were employed together with other non-Muslim minority groups on an equal basis with their Muslim colleagues in these institutions in a complete spirit of co-operation as a team. They performed commendable services according to their qualifications as members of the health profession and received no discrimination on account of their faith.[154]

These are but a few glimpses of the Muslims' contribution to hospitals. A careful perusal of the contribution reveals the fact that the modern world is highly indebted to the outstanding efforts which Muslims made for the development of this institution over several centuries, when they were in the vanguard of world civilisation. The contemporary world has never witnessed a parallel progress but has benefited notably from this contribution. European lords frequently visited well equipped and developed hospitals of Muslim Spain in order to be treated.

It is interesting to note that the first European mental hospital was built in the 15th century C.E. at Valencia in Spain by the Brothers of St. John. This European institution was based on a similar institution in Cairo and modelled on the Bimaristan of Baghdad. The same Brothers were later summoned to France by Marie de Medicito to build psychiatric hospitals at Charenton and the Charite at Senlis.[155]

The Development of Hospitals in the Muslim World

"The story of hospitals in Islam", says S.K. Hamarneh, "reveals some unusual facts regarding their rise in Arabic States and their development which surpassed all previous accomplishments of the kind in recorded history."[156]

Kaysari hospital and medical school in 1206 AD (Turkey).

Hospitals' Day to Day Routine

The Development of Hospitals in the Muslim World

Hospitals' Day to Day Routine

Attempts were always made to construct hospitals in the most hygienic parts of the city. It is interesting to note the method which Abū Bakr Zakariya al-Rāzī adopted when he was asked to select a new site for the state hospital at Baghdad, of which he was the chief physician. He suggested that an animal should be slaughtered and shreds of its meat be hung in different areas. The area where these shreds showed the least sign of putrefaction should be chosen as the site of the hospital.[157] Likewise attempts were made to keep the hospital and its surroundings clean. For this purpose cleaners, both male and female, were appointed and granted good salaries. Hospitals were not commissioned unless adequate arrangements were made for their smooth running over several years. Caliphs always instructed the hospital authorities to treat patients with absolute kindness. Some of them would even visit the hospitals personally and carry out an inspection.

Hospitals were divided into two principal wards: male and female. Each section was further divided into wards in view of the different kinds of diseases. Surgeons and physicians were appointed to each ward with a head specialist physician or surgeon. Above each sectional head there was a Director, *Mu'tawallī/Tīmārdār.* This post was given to the physician of greatest repute. Attempts were made to invite twice or thrice a week reputed physicians from the city for consultation regarding complicated cases. Each hospital had a *saydaliyyah* pharmacy and was known as *khazānat al-sharāb.* The post of Inspector General of Hospitals was created during the 'Abbāsid regime, and was usually occupied by the most outstanding physicians of the Islamic world. The post of Chief Chemist was also created. The main function of this officer was the development of the pharmacy pharmacy and supervision for the preparation of drugs in the pharmacy. For example, Diya' ibn Bayṭār who was a great botanist and herbalist of his time occupied this post in 646/1248. The State established a special Health department for the Public Health and handsome funds were allocated for this purpose. Expert and experienced physicians were appointed to head this department both for its smooth running as well as seeking their advice from time to time.

Once a physician had examined a person and determined that they be admitted to the hospital for treatment, the patient was first taken to the bathroom where his clothes were removed and deposited in a special room. Until his recovery, he was provided with hospital apparel and taken to a ward befitting his sickness and given a comfortable bed. In some well-equipped hospitals each patient was assigned an attendant whose assignment was to look after the comfort, food, diet, medicine and other needs of the patient. In case of need, physicians were called from other wards for mutual consultation and in an emergency a patient could be transferred to a special ward.

The doors of the hospitals were open for all citizens without discrimination of race, colour, nationality or religion. The hospital facilities were shared equally by all patients. All cured patients were issued new clothing and money from hospital funds to sustain them until they found suitable work. The hospitals also provided free funeral services for patients who died on their premises.

The hospital store had lawful beverages, fine varieties of creams, sumptuous jams, varieties of medicine and striking essences which were not found elsewhere. It also contained surgical instruments, glass jars, curdled milk, etc. There were special sections for cooking, cleaning and administration.

The celebrated hospitals were provided with teaching facilities. A huge lecture theatre was constructed in each hospital which was then fully equipped with medical instruments. Students used to sit in front of their lecturers. Lectures were delivered after a practical study of the patients' diseases. At times both students and lecturers were engaged in useful discussions on different topics of medicine.

It is also interesting to note that monkeys were used for medical research. In 222/836 the ruler of Nubia was ordered to supply a particular species of ape said to resemble man very closely.[158]

The Development of Hospitals in the Muslim World

Discussions around the bedside was a common teaching practice. Razi writes in the opening chapter of his book *Bari' al-sā'ah*, (*Cure within the Hour*):

I was once in the company of Abul Qāsim ibn 'Abd Allāh. In his presence were general qualified practitioners and others who were still seekinggraduation.Each of these joined in the discussion according to the depth of his knowledge.[159]

Medical students' knowledge and aptitude were asertained by expert physicians, using the patients and the hospitals' equipments. Successful students were awarded certificates.

Well established hospital libraries, provided ample opportunites for both students and physicians to consult books from their extremely rich collections. Files were kept in which the ailment, the medicine, the diet and the progress was recorded of each patient.

Health Science and Human Dignity

Muslims generally used the word *ḥakīm* for a physician. Three other prominent Muslim languages - Persian, Urdu and Turkish - use the word for the same meaning. There is a great significance attached for the use of this Arabic word. The word *hakim* is derived form *ḥakama* which literary means to pass a judgement, express an opinion and *ḥakīm* on the measure of *fā'il* is an active particle it means 'one who performs, or executes, affairs firmly, solidly, soundly, thoroughly, skillfully, judiciously or well'.[162] All attributes mentioned in the meaning are highly essential because a person puts his health - the most precious treasure of his/her life - in the hands of a physician. Naturally the selection of such an indispensible person should be based on wisdom and great care.

The jurisdiction of human dignity governs human life. Any negligence on the part of a person would mean the loss of a life which is considered by the Qur'ān as killing entire mankind.

Muslim physicians, *ḥukamā* never isolated soul from human physical body. It is spirituality which Muslims believe governs human soul. This belief is based on the Qur'ān. A number of *adhkār*, remembrance of Allah which the Qur'ān prescribes grant mental peace. Whenever Muslims turned to physicians they always expected cure for both spheres of their life soul and body. It is interesting to quote here a ninth century C.E physician Ishaq bin 'Ali Rahawi, who wrote probably the first treatise on *Adab al-Ṭabīb*. A substantial part of this treatise, based on a unique Arabic manuscript found in Turkey has been translated by Martin Levy under the title 'Medical Ethics of Medieval Islam with special Reference to Rahawi's "Practical Ethics of the Physician". Rahawi treats physicians as 'guardians of souls and bodies'[163] and emphasises inter relationship of the spiritual and bodily physic.[164] Keeping in mind this dual role of physicians and expectations of their patients for the cure of both ailments increase considerably the responsibility of physicians in Muslim society. It clearly means that a morally bankrupt physician shall not be accepted by the Muslim society. The success of physicians in their profession always depends on their knowledge, competence, skill of health science and sublime moral character. These characteristics were responsible factors for the spread of name and fame of physicians and promotion of patient physician responsibility.

It is essential, Rahawi believes, for a physician to have unshakable faith in Allah[165] and He alone as a Healer. The physician must be honest in his profession. He should not treat a patient when he is uncertain concerning the ailment.[166]

The treatment of a sick person is a great responsibility on the shoulder of a physician and he is accountable for this responsibility. For the discharge of this duty Rahawi strongly recommends maintaining a daily chart of all medical issues of each patient. The chart can be retained in case of recovery of the patient for future reference as a medical record. In case of the death of a patient the chart can save the physician, provided there is no discripency in the treatment, from capital punishment for killing a human being.[167]

Ishaq bin 'Ali Rahawi gives the principal aim for writing his *Adab al-Tabib*, he writes:

"[it is] to strengthen the souls of physicians about the truths. Thereby they can repel evil practices in the treatment of healthy and ill, hoping for rewards and trusting in the help of the exalted God and His support for him.
Thus, I have undertaken in this book, as much as I can, to collect material about the ethics which a physician must cultivate, and the manner in which the physician must strengthen his moral character."[168]

The book includes the following chapters:[169]

Chapter I

On the loyalty and faith in which a physician must believe, and on the ethics which he must follow.

Chapter II

On the means and measures by which a physician treats his own body and limbs. This part includes many duties which must be discussed in detail.

Chapter III

On things of which a physician must beware.

Chapter IV

On the directions which a physician must give to the patients and servants.

Chapter V

On the behaviour of the patient's visitors.

Chapter VI

On simple and compound drugs which a physician must consider and on his remedial directions which may be corrupted by the pharmacist and others.

Chapter VII

On matters of which a physician must question the patient or others.

Chapter VIII

On the necessity for ill and healthy people to have faith in the physicians and the outcome when it is annulled.

Chapter IX

On the agreement that the patient must follow the directions of the physicians and the outcome when it is annulled.

Chapter X

On the behaviour of the patient with his people and servants.

Chapter XI

On the behaviour of the patient in regard to his visitors.

Chapter XII

On the dignity of the medical profession.

Chapter XIII

On that people must respect a physician according to his skill but kings and other honourable men must respect him more. It is necessary to honour him above royalty and virtuous people.

Chapter XIV

Peculiar incidents concerning physicians, that is those already known, so that the physician may be forewarned. Some are funny and may help him to discover uncooperative persons before the consultation lest he be held responsible for any harm that may occur.

Chapter XV

On the subject that not everyone may practice the profession of medicine but that it must be practiced by those who have suitable nature and moral character.

Chapter XVI

On examination of physicians.

Chapter XVII

On ways by which kings may remove corruption of physicians and guide the people in regard to medicine, and how it was in ancient times.

Chapter XVIII

On the necessity of warning against quacks who call themselves physicians and the difference between their deceit and the true medical art.

Chapter XIX

On faulty habits to which people are accustomed but which may injure both the sick and healthy and cause physicians to be blamed.

Chapter XX

On matters which a physician must observe and be careful about during periods of health in order to prepare for periods of illness and at the time of youth for old age.

The medical oath of a Muslim physician which is prepared from the historical and contemporary writings of physicians of the Islamic World and its official adoption by the Islamic Medical association (IMA) in 1977 bears clear testimony that the legacy for the promotion of human dignity in health science is a continuous practice among Muslim physicians of all generations.

Praise be to Allah (God), the Teacher, the Unique, Majesty of the Heavens ,
the Exalted, the Glorious, Glory be to Him, the Eternal Being Who created the
Universe and all the creatures within, and the only Being Who containeth the
infinity and the eternity. we serve no other god besides Thee .....
Give us the wisdom to comfort and counsel all towards peace and harmony.

Give us the understanding that ours is a profession sacred that deals with your most precious gifts of life and intellect.
Therefore, make us worthy of this favoured station with honour, dignity and piety so that we may devote our lives in serving mankind, poor or rich, literate or illiterate, Muslim or non-Muslim , black or white with patience and tolerance with virtue and reverence, with knowledge and vigilance, with Thy love in our hearts and compassion for Thy servants, Thy most precious creation.
hereby we take this oath in Thy name, the Creator of all the Heavens and the earth and follow Thy counsel as Thou hast revealed to Prophet Muḥammad (pbuh).

"Whoever killeth a human being, not in lieu of another human being nor because of mischief on earth, it is as if he hath killed all mankind. And if he saveth a human life, he hath saved the life of all mankind."
(The Qur'an 5:32)[170]

The Development of Hospitals in the Muslim World

Conclusion

Conclusion

During the time of the Prophet, most Muslims were illiterate. Due to the painstaking and ceaseless efforts of the Prophet, many became literate. The Prophet's policy of free universal education for both the sexes, provided an opportunity for people from the common strata to adorn themselves with the jewels of knowledge. Very soon the world witnessed remarkable progress in Muslim scholarship which did not discriminate between religious and secular education. To Muslims, religion cannot be treated as a separate entity. All aspects of life are integral parts of religion. This is because Islam governs a Muslims' life from the cradle to the grave. This spirit and attitude opened many avenues for Muslims. They were able to assimilate the world's heritage through translations in Arabic and, to equip themselves with the contributions made so far in Cosmology, Cosmography, Geography, Natural History, Physics, Mathematics, Astronomy, Medicine, Chemistry, Philosophy and other sciences. Later, they utilised their own genius in order to make critical and original contributions to existing fields of study, introducing new disciplines of knowledge on sound scientific principles which helped tremendously in the progress of many fields in Western civilisation.

Mere spiritual progress at the cost of worldly progress is not recognised in Islam; nor is worldly progress to the exclusion of spiritual upliftment accepted.

Seyyed Hossein Nasr says:

> Islamic science, by contrast, seeks ultimately to attain such knowledge as will contribute towards the spiritual perfection and deliverance of anyone capable of studying it.[160]

The great emphasis which two authoritative sources place on the protection of human life and provisions for its welfare are such that it is possible for a human being to live in peace, justice and mutual cooperation retaining dignity and honour.

The broad principles from the sources concerning health, hygiene and sickness were granted to mankind some fourteen hundred years ago but their utility, natural and practical wisdom cannot be ignored in this modern age of science and technology. One of the greatest contributions of the Prophet was that he not only translated them practically in his life but he also made them an integral part of the *Sharī'ah*, Islamic Law.

If one could open a window of the Muslim hospitals mentioned in Section III and from there look at any well organised modern hospital one would find similarities in their working routine for the care and comfort of ailing people.

Hospitals were constructed at the most hygienic sites. These buildings were spacious and lavishly decorated, and well equipped and accommodated in their courtyards were orchards and beautiful gardens with fountains.

It is gratifying to observe that the development of hospitals was largely based on Islamic principles while the decisive influence of Islamic teachings can easily be traced in their all-round development. Handsome public endowment funds were established by Muslims for the maintenance of hospitals and these turned the hospitals into charitable institutions in the service of Allah, making facilities available to all sections of mankind. Celebrated hospitals became the seat of medical knowledge and research centres and contributed immensely to the progress of the science of medicine. All such practical measures were taken by Muslims with great zeal and dedication so that patients received maximum comfort and effective cures on the basis of the recognition of the dignity, honour and equality of all human beings.

As the boundaries of the world are rapidly shrinking, there is a pressing need to bridge the gulf between the East and the West. We are optimistic that Islam will not disappoint people, if they sincerely use it for this purpose. A Western Professor of Arabic Sir Hamilton Gibb, shares our optimism in his book *Whither Islam*:

Islam has a still further service to render to the cause of humanity.

The Development of Hospitals in the Muslim World

**It stands after all nearer to the real East than Europe does,
and it possesses a magnificent tradition of inter-racial understanding
and cooperation. No other society has such a record of success
in uniting in an equality of status of opportunity, and endeavour
so many and so various races of mankind.... Islam has still the power to
reconcile apparently irreconcilable elements of race and tradition.**[161]

References

1. George Sarton, Lecturer on Islam, Middle East Institute, quoted by S. Cobb in *Islamic Contribution to Civilisation,* p.47 (the italics are mine for emphasis).
2. Under the doctrine; three basic Qur'anic themes, e.g. *al-Tawḥīd,* Oneness of Allah, *al-Risàlah,* Prophethood and *al-Ākhirah'* the life hereafter, one or all three can easily be traced from the 114 *Sūrahs,* chapters of the Qur'ān.
3. The Qur'ān, **2** : 164, 171, 229, 266, **3** :191; **6** : 50, 65, 98; **7** : 176,179; **8** : 22; **10** : 24; **13** : 3, 4, 8; **16** : 11, 12, 67; **17**:44; **22** : 46; **23** : 68, **30** : 8, 18, 24 ; **36** : 68; **39** : 42; **45** : 5, 13; **59** : 21 and many more.
4. *Ibid,* **41** : 53.
5. *Ibid,* **2** : 259; **5** : 75; **6** : 65; **7** : 103, 185; **12** : 109; **30** : 9; **35** : 44;**50** : 6; **80** : 24; **86** : 5.
6. *Ibid* ., **35** : 28.
7. *Ibid.* , **58** : 11.
8. Al- Tirmidhi, *'Ilm,* 19; Ibn Mājah, *Zuhd,* 15.
9. The Qur'ān vehemently condemns the concealment of knowledge: "Those who hide the proofs and guidance which We have revealed, after We had made it clear in the Scripture, such are accursed of Allah and accursed of those who have the power to curse" (**2** : 159).
10. Ibn Mājah, *Muqaddimah,* 17.

11a. Isfihānī, *Ḥilyat al-Awliyā' wa Ṭabaqāt al-Aṣfiyā,* vol. i, p. 337, Cairo, 1351 A.H; al- Maqrīzī, *al- Khiṭaṭ,* vol. iv, p. 293.

11b. *Making of Humanity,* p.188.

12. Seyyed Hossein Nasr, *An Introduction to Islamic Cosmological Doctrines,* p.174.
13. S. Ali, *Intellectual Foundation of Islamic Civilization* ,.p.35.

14 Al-Ghazālī, *Iḥyā 'Ulūm al-Dīn, The Book of Knowledge,* p.26.

15 *Ibid.,* p. 130.

16. *Ibid.*, p. 23.17.
17. *Ibid.*, p. 201.
18. *Ibid.*, p. 219.
19. *Ibid.*, p. 201.
20. *Ibid.*, pp. 203-4.
21. *Ibid.*, p. 146.
22 *Ibid.*, p. 59.
23. *Ibid.*, p. 156.
24. *Ibid.*, p. 56.
25. *Ibid* , p. 147-8.
26. *The Making of Humanity,* pp. 20-1.
27. *A Short History of Muslim Culture,* quoted by A.K. Ali, Lahore,p.58.
28. *Ibid.*, pp. 95-6.
29. *Ibid.*, p. 55.
30. See, for a very interesting account of the variety of occupations of the 14,000 Muslim Jurists and Traditionalists and the secular occupations of Muslim Jurisprudents and Traditionalists in the classical period of Islam, *The Economic and Social History of the Orient,* xiii (1970), pp.16-61.
31. Baron Carra de Vaux, in *The Legacy of Islam,* p. 377.
32. Helmots, *History of the World* quoted by S. Cobb, *Islamic Contribution to Civilisation* , p. 32.
33. *Arabic Literature,* p. 4
34. *A Guide to the History of Science,* p.29.
36. The Qur'ān, **6** : 162.
35. H.R.H The Prince of Wales, *Islam in the West,* p. 17.
37. *Ibid.,* **5** : 32.
38. A Divine saying put in the words of the Prophet.
39. *al-Jāmiʿ al-Ṣaḥīḥ,* Muslim, *al-Birr,* 25
40. For a brief account see my booklet, *Islam: The Qur'anic Overview,* pp.14-20.
41. *Ibid.,* **89** : 28.42.
42. The Qur'ān, **89** : 27.

References

43. *Ibid.*, **89** : 28.
44. *Ibid.*, **2** : 30.
45. *Ibid.*, **31** : 20.
46. *al-Jāmiʿ al-Ṣaḥīḥ,* Muslim, *Jihād,* 2; Abū Dāwūd, *Sunan, Jihād,* 82; al-Tirmidhī, *al-Jāmiʿ al-Ṣaḥīḥ, Siyar,* 48; Ibn Mājah, *Sunan, Jihād,* 38; al-Dārimī, *Sunan, Siyar,* 5; *Muwaṭṭa', Jihād,* 11; Aḥmad ibn Ḥanbal, *Musnad,* **1** : 300, **4** : 240, **5** : 358.
47. M.N. al-Nasīmī, *al-Ṭibb al-Nabawī wa 'Ilm al-Ḥadīth,* vol. iii, p. 31.
48. Muwatta', *Janā'iz,* 45, Abū Dāwūd, *Sunan, Janā'iz,* 60; Ibn Mājah, *Sunan, Janā'iz,* 63; Aḥmad ibn Ḥanbal, **6** : 58, 100.
49. *al-Ṭibb al-Nabī wa 'Ilm al-Ḥadīth, op. cit.* vol. iii, p. 31
50. *Ibid.*
51. al-Tirmidhī, *al-Jāmiʿ al-Ṣaḥīḥ, Tafsīr Sūrah,* 49, *Manāqib,* 73; Abū Dāwūd, *Sunan, Adab,* 111; Aḥmad ibn Ḥanbal, **2** : 261, 524.
52. Aḥmad ibn Ḥanbal, **5** : 411.
53. *The Qur'ān,* **49** : 13. *al-Jāmiʿal-Ṣaḥīḥ, al-Bukhārī, Anbiyā,*54; *Maghāzī,* 53, *Ḥudūd, al-Jāmiʿal Ṣaḥīḥ, Muslim, Ḥudūd,* 9; *Abū Dāwūd, Sunan, Ḥudūd,* 4; *al-Jāmiʿal-Ṣaḥīḥ, al-Tirmidhī, Ḥudūd,* 6; *Ibn Mājah, Sunan, Ḥudūd,* 6.
54. *al-Ṭabarī,* ii, pp. 450, 1319, 1802; Ibn Hishām, iv, p. 311; Abū Yūsuf, *Kitāb al-Kharāj,* p. 110.
56. The Qur'ān, **49** : 13.
57. *Ibid.*, **67** : 1-2.
58. *al-Jāmiʿ al-Ṣaḥīḥ*, al-Bukhārī, *al-Ṣawm,* 55, *al-Nikāḥ,* 89, *Adab,* 84; *al-Jamiʿ al-Ṣaḥīḥ,* Muslim, *al-Ṣiyām,* 183, 193; al-Nasā'ī, *Sunan, al-Ṣiyām,* 84.
59. *al-Jāmiʿ al-Ṣaḥīḥ,* Muslim, *al-Qadr,* 34; Ibn Mājah, *Sunan, al-Muqaddimah,* 1, *al-Zuhd,* 14; *Aḥmad ibn Hanbal,* **3** : 316, 370.
60. The Qur'ān, **13** : 11.
61. *Ibid.*, **55** : 39.
62. *Ibid.*, **28** : 77.
63. *Ibid.*, **67** : 15.
64. *Ibid.*, **14** : 34.

65. *Ibid.*, **5** : 8; **49** : 9; **60** : 8; **3** : 18.
66. *Ibid.*, **2** : 143.
67. *Ibid.*, **6** : 141; **7** : 31; **17** : 26, 27.
68. *Ibid.*, **2** : 173; **5** : 3-6; **6** : 38, 121; **5** : 96; **16** : 4.
69. As-Suyūtī's, *Medicine of the Prophet,* quoted from al-Nasa'ī, *Sunan* and al-Tirmidhī, *al-Jāmi' al-Ṣaḥīḥ,* p.11.
70. As-Suyūtī's, *Medicine of the Prophet,* quoted from *al-Jami' al-Sahih,* al-Tirmidhī and Ibn Mājah, *Sunan,* p. 13.
71. As-Suyūtī's, *Medicine of the Prophet,* quoted from Abu Nu'aym, p. 13.
72. *The Qur'ān,* **5** : 90.
73. al-Nasā'ī, *Sunan, Ashribah,* 44.
74. As-Suyūtī's, *Medicine of the Prophet,* quoted from *al-Jāmi' al-Ṣaḥīḥ,* Muslim, p. 14.
75. As-Suyūti's, *Medicine of the Prophet,* quoted from a*l-Jāmi' al-Ṣaḥiḥ,* al-Bukhārī, p. 15.
76. *The Qur'ān,* **2** :13; **4** : 4, 6; **7** : 24; **30** : 21.
77. *The Qur'ān,* **2** : 222.
78. *al-Jāmi' al-Ṣaḥīḥ,* al-Bukhārī, *Riqāq,*1; al-Tirmidhī, *al-Jāmi' al-Ṣaḥīḥ, Zuhd,* 1; Ibn Mājah, *Sunan, Zuhd,* 15; al-Dārimī, *Sunan, Riqāq,* 2.
79. *The Qur'ān,* **74** : 5.
80. *Ibid.*, **7** : 131.
81. *Ibid.*, **6** : 41.
82. *Ibid.*, **7** : 32.
83. *al-Jāmi' al-Ṣaḥīḥ,* Muslim, *al-'Īmān,* 147; Ibn Mājah, *Sunan, al-Du'ā,'* 10; Aḥmad ibn Ḥanbal, *Musnad,* **4** : 133, 134, 151.
84. *al-Jāmi' al-Ṣaḥīḥ,* Muslim, *Jumu'ah,* 7; Abū Dāwūd, *Sunan, Ṭahārah,* 127; al-Nasā'ī, *Sunan, Jumu'ah,* 6; Aḥmad ibn Ḥanbal, *Musnad,* **3** : 30, 66, 69, 81; **4** : 34; **5** : 198, 438, 440.
85. *The Qur'ān,* **5** : 6.
86. *Ibid.*
87. *Ibid.*
88. *al-Jāmi' al-Ṣaḥīḥ,* al-Bukhārī, *Libās,* 63, 64; *al-Jāmi' al-Ṣaḥīḥ,* Muslim, *Ṭahārah,* 49; Abū Dāwūd, *Sunan, Ṭahārah,* 29 ; *al-Jāmi' al-Ṣaḥīḥ,*

al-Tirmidhī, *Adab*, 14; al-Nasā'ī, *Sunan, Ṭahārah*, 9, 10; Ibn Mājah, *Sunan, Ṭahārah*, 8.

89. *al-Jāmi' al-Ṣaḥīḥ,* Muslim.

90. *al-Jāmi' al-Ṣaḥīḥ,* al-Tirmidhī, *Adab*, 41.

91. *al-Jāmi' al-Ṣaḥīḥ,* al-Bukhārī, *al-Ṭibb*, 53, 54; *al-Jāmi' al-Ṣaḥīḥ,* Muslim, *al-Ṣawm*, 104; Abū Dāwūd, *Sunan, al-Ṭibb*, 24; Ibn Mājah, *Sunan, al-Ṭibb*, 43.

92. Aḥmad ibn Ḥanbal, *Musnad,* **1** : 178, 180; **3** : 416; **4** : 177, 186; **5** : 206, 208, 210, 273.

93. Ibn Qayyim al-Jawziyyah, *The Prophetic Medicine*, quoted from *al-Jāmi' al-Ṣaḥīḥ,* of al-Bukhārī and Muslim, p. 139.

94. *The Qur'ān,* **26** : 80.

95. *Ibid.*, **2** : 156.

96. *al-Jāmi' al-Ṣaḥīḥ,* al-Bukhārī, *Marḍā*, 3; *al-Jāmi' al-Ṣaḥīḥ,* Muslim, *Birr*, 46, 47, 48; *al-Jāmi' al-Ṣaḥīḥ,* al-Tirmidhī, *Janā'iz*,1; Muwaṭṭa', *'Ayn*, 6; Aḥmad ibn Ḥanbal, **1** : 441; **3** : 23; **4** : 56; **6** : 39, 42, 43, 160, 173-5; As-Suyūṭī's, *Medicine of the Prophet,* p. 177.

97. As-Suyūṭī's, *Medicine of the Prophet,* p.125.

98. Abū Dāwūd, *Sunan, Ṭibb*, 1; Aḥmad ibn Ḥanbal, **3** : 156.

99. Ibn Qayyim al-Jawziyyah, *The Prophetic Medicine,* p. 130, quoted from Abū Dāwūd and al-Nasā'ī, *Sunans* and *al-Jāmi' al-Ṣaḥīḥ,* Ibn Mājah.

100. As-Suyūṭī's, *Medicine of the Prophet,* p. 123.

101. There are a few works already published on this theme:Ibn Qayyim al-Jawziyyah, *The Prophetic Medicine*; As-Suyūṭī's, *Medicine of the Prophet*; Al-Bar, M.A., *Hal Hunāka Ṭibbu Nabawī;* al-Nasīmī, *Al-Ṭibb-un-Nabawī,* 'Abdul Hameed, H., *The Holy Prophet as a Healer*, A.H. Basalamah,'The Philosophy in Tibb Nabawi'; H.M. Chisti, 'Applications of Tibb-i-Nabi to Modern Medical Practice'; H 'Ata-ur-Rehman,'Tibb-e-Nabavi'; Ghaznawī, K., *Ṭibb-i-Nabawi Awr Jadīd Science.*

102. al-Tirmidhi, *al-Jāmi 'al- Ṣaḥīḥ, al-Adab,* 1; al-Nasā'ī, *Sunan, al-Janā'iz,* 52; Ibn Mājah, *Sunan, al-Janā'iz,* 1; al-Dārimī, *Sunan, al-Istī'zān,* **6** : 216; Aḥmad ibn Ḥanbal, *Musnad,* **4** : 284.

103. Malik, *al-Muwaṭṭa', al-'Ayn,* 17.
104. Aḥmad ibn Ḥanbal, *Musnad,* 1 : 97, 5 : 368.
105. *al-Jāmi 'al-Ṣaḥiḥ,* al-Bukhārī.
106. *al-Jāmi'al- Ṣaḥīḥ,* al-Bukhārī, *Marḍā,* 20; Aḥmad ibn Ḥanbal, *Musnad,* **4** : 284.
107. *As-Suyūtī's, Medicine of the Prophet,* quoted from *al-Jāmi 'al- Ṣaḥīḥ,* al-Bukhārī, p. 179.
108. *Ibid.,* p. 180.
109. al-Bukhārī has included in his *al-Jāmi 'al-Ṣaḥīḥ* a special chapter on this theme: *'Ayādat al-Marīḍ,* 1.
110. *al-Jāmi 'al- Ṣaḥīḥ,* al-Bukhārī, *Tafsīr Sūrah,* 59, *Adab,* 9; Ibn Mājah, *Sunan, Zuhd,* 13; Abū Dāwūd, *Sunan,* 6; Aḥmad ibn Ḥanbal, *Musnad,* 4 : 47, 48, 50.
111. al-Sarakhsī, *al-Mabsūṭ,* Cairo, 1324 A.H., vol. xii, p.27; al-Marghīnānī, Burhān al-Dīn, *al-Hidāyah,* Karachi, vol. ii, p. 637 quoted by Tanzīl-ur-Rahmān, *A Code of Muslim Personal Law,* vol. ii, p. 101.
112. *Ibid.*
113. A.A.A. Fayzee, *Outlines of Muhammadan Law,* third edition, p. 266.
114. al-Bukhārī, *Ṣalāh,* 77.
115. al-Ṭabarī, *Ta'rīkh al-Umam wal Mulūk,* vol. viii,. p. 97, quoted by Hamarneh *Health Sciences in Early Islam,* 1983, vol. i, p. 97.
116. C. Elgood., *A Medical History of Persia,* p. 70.
117. Mayerhofmax, *Von Alexandien nach Baghdad.* Translated by A.R. Badwī. *al-Turāth al-Yūnānī Ḥaḍārat al-Islāmiyah,* p. 57.
118. Ibn Nadím, *al-Fihrist ,* p. 245.
119. al-Qiftī, *Ikhbār al-'Ulamā' bi Akhbār al-Ḥukamā',* p. 133.
120. Ibn Abī Usaybī'ah Abū Dāwūd Sulaymān bin Ḥassan, *Ṭabaqāt al-Aṭibbā' wal Ḥukamā',* vol. 1, p. 222.
121. Ibn Abī Usaybī'ah, vol.1, p. 222; al-Qiftī, p. 191 quoted by P.K. Hitti, *History of the Arabs,* p. 364. See also Ahmad 'Īsā, *Ta'rīkh al-Bīmāristānāt fil Islām,* Beirut, p .57 and Abū al-Faraj Bar Hebraeus, *Ta'rīkh Mukhtaṣar al-Duwal,* ed. A.Salihānī, Beirut, 1890, pp. 281-2.
122. al-Sibā'ī, Muṣtafa, *Min Rawā'i Haḍāratinā al-Islāmiyyah,* p. 141.

References

123. *Ibid.*
124. Ibn Abī Usaybī'ah *Ṭabaqat al-Aṭibbā wal Ḥukamā'*, .vol. 1,p. 234.
125. *Ibid.*
126. Ibn Taghri Birdi, *al-Nujūm al-Zāhirah fi Mulūk Miṣr wal Qāhirah*, ed. T.G.J. Juynboll, vol ii, p. 11.
127. Maqrīzī, *Khiṭaṭ*. vol. vii, p. 405.
128. *Ṭib al-'Arab*, translation of *Arabian Medicine* by E.G. Brown by N.A.A. Wāstī with explanation and criticism, p. 448.
129. 'Īsā Aḥmad, Bak, , *Ta'rīkh al-Bimāristānāt fil Islām*, p.29.
130. al-Qiftī, *Ikhbār al-Ulamā' bi Akhbār al-Ḥukamā'*, p.p. 235-6,337-8, 438; Ibn Abī Usaybī'ah, *Ṭabaqāt*, vol. 1 pp. 238, 244, 310.
131. Ibn Batuta, *Tuḥfat al-Nuzzār*, vol.1, p. 134, Cairo 1871, quoted by Hamarneh in *Health Sciences in Early Islam*, vol. i, p. 110.
132. Ibn Jubayr, *Riḥlāt ibn Jubayr*, Gibb Memorial Series, vol. v, pp. 325-6, Leiden, 1949.
133. C.Elgood *A Medical History of Persia and the Eastern Caliphate*, quoted on, p. 159.
134. Ice at that time was expensive and beyond the reach of common people because it was brought to the cities with great effort from the mountains.
135. See Ibn Abī Usaybi'ah, *Ṭabaqāt al-Aṭibbā*, vol ii, *Ṭib Islāmī*, p. 450.
136. quoted by Wasti in *Tib al-'Arab*, pp. 450-1.
137. Wasti, *Tib al-'Arab*, p. 451; *Min Raw'ai Hadaratina*, pp. 144-5.
138. Ibn Abī Usaybī'ah, *Ṭabaqāt*, vol. iii, pp. 256-7.
139. *Riḥlāt ibn Jubayr*, pp. 283-4.
140. Hasan 'Abd al-Wahhāb, al-Ṭib al-'Arabī fī Afrīqiyyah, *al-Fikr*, 1985, vol. 3, no. 10, pp. 907-16.quoted by Hamarneh in *Health Sciences*, p. 100.
141. C. Elgood, *A Medical History of Persia*, pp. 176-7.
142. Jurji Zaydān, *Ta'rīkh al Tamaddun al-Islāmī*, vol. III p. 188, quoted in *Ṭib al-'Arab*, p. 451.
143. Wastī, *Ṭib al-'Arab*, p. 452.
144. *Ibid.*
145. C.Elgood , *A Medical History of Persia*, p. 172.

146. al-Maqrizī, *Mawā'iz al-I'tibār bi Dhikr al-Khiṭaṭ wal-Āthār*, vol. ii, p. 405.
147. Zaydān Jurjī, *Ta'rīkh al-Tamaddun al-Islāmī*, vol. iii, p. 188.
148. al-Maqrizī, *al-Khiṭaṭ*, vol. ii, p. 405.
149. *Min Rawāi' Ḥadāratinā*, p. 145.
150. Wāstī, *Ṭib al-'Arab*, p. 454.
151. *Ibid.*
152. al-Maqrizī, *al-Khiṭaṭ*, vol. ii , pp. 406-407.
153. Hamarneh, *Health Sciences in Early Islam,* p. 102.
154. *Ibid.*, p. 105.
155. S.H.Z. Naqui, 'Islam and Development of Science', *Nigerian Journal of Islam*, vol. i, p. 5, (1971-72).
156. Hamarneh, *Health Sciences in Early Islam,* p. 104.
157. *Min Rawāi' Ḥadāratinā,* p. 145.
158. P.K. Hitti, *History of the Arabs*, p. 146.
159. *Ibid.*, p. 36(3.
160. S.H. Nasr, *Science and Civilization in Islam*, p. 39.
161. H.A.R. Gibb, *Whither Islam*, p. 379.
162. E.Lane, *Arabic-English Lexicon*
163. M.Levy, 'Medical ethics of Mediecval Islam with Special Reference to Ruhawi's "Practical Ethics of the Physician', *The American Philosophical Society*, p. 8.
164. *Ibid.,* p. 9.
165. *Ibid.,* p. 10.
166. *Ibid.,* p. 11.
167. *Ibid.,*
168. *Ibid.,* p. 12.
169. *Ibid.,* pp. 18-9.
170. S. Athar (ed.), *Islamic Perspectives in Medicine*, p. 195.

Bibliography

Abdul Hameed, Hakim, *The Holy Prophet as a Healer*, Institute of History of Medicine and Medical Research, New Delhi, 1977.

Anees, M., (Ed.), *Health Sciences in Early Islam*, Noor Health Foundation and Zahra Publications, Texas, 1983.

Aḥmad ibn Ḥanbal, *Musnad.*

Ahmad, N., *Muslim Contribution to Geography*, Sh. Muhammad Ashraf,Lahore, 1972.

Ali, A.K., *A Short History of Muslim Culture*, Lahore, 1962.

Ali, S., *Intellectual Foundation of Islamic Civilization*, Publishers United Ltd, Lahore, 1977.

Arberry, A.J., *Aspects of Islamic Civilization As Depicted in the Original Texts*, George Allen & Unwin Ltd., London, 1964.

'Ata-ur-Rehman, Hakim, '*Tibb-e-Nabawi.' Hamdard* 3 (1-2) : 101-19, (1959).

Athar, S., (Ed.), *Islamic Perspective in Medicine, A Survey of Islamic Medicine: Achievements and Contemporary Issues*, American Trust Publications, Indianapolis, 1993.

al-Baihaqī, *Shu'bat al'-Īmān.*

Bakhsh, S.K. and Margoliouth, D.S., (Trans), *The Renaissance of Islam*, Kitab Bhavan, Delhi, 1979.

Bammate, H., *Muslim Contribution to Civilization,* American Trust Publications, Indiana, 1976.

Bamborough, P., *Treasures of Islam,* Blandford Press, Dorset, 1976.

Bak, Aḥmad 'Īsā, *Ta'rīkh al-Bīmāristānāt fil Islām*, Damascus, 1939.

al-Bār, M.A., *Hal Hunāka Ṭibbu Nabawī,* Al-Dār-Sa'ūdiyyah, Jeddah, 1988.

Baron Carra De Vaux, The Legacy of Islam, Oxford, 1931.

Basalamah, A.H., 'The Philosophy in Tibb Nabawi.' *Journal of Islamic Medical Association,* (USA), 14 (1-2) :21-2.

Ibn Baṭūṭa, *Tuḥfat al-Nuzzār*, Cairo, 1871.

Blunt, W., *Splendours of Islam*, Angus & Robertson, London, 1976.

Boisard, M.A., *Humanity in Islam*, American Trust Publications, Indiana, 1988.

Bosworth C.E.. The Islamic Dynasties, Edinburgh University, 1967.

Briffault R., *Making of Humanity.*

Brown, E.G., *Arabian Medicine*, University Press, Cambridge, 1962.

al-Bukhārī, *al-Jāmi' al-Ṣaḥīḥ.*

Burckhardt, T., *Art of Islam: Language and Meaning*, World of Islam Festival Publishing Company Ltd., England, 1976.

Chishti, H.M., 'Applications of Tibb-i-Nabi to Modern Medical Practice', *Journal of Islamic Medical Association* (USA), 11 (1-2):1825, (1980).

Cobb, S., *Islamic Contributions to Civilization*, Avalon Press, Washington D.C., 1965.

al-Dārimī, *Sunan.*

Abū Dāwūd, *Sunan.*

Dodge, B., *Al-Azhar: A Millennium of Muslim Learning*, The Middle EasInstitute, Washington, D.C., 1961.

Dunlop, D.M., *Arab Civilization to AD 1500,* Longman Group Limited, London, 1971.

Ibn Abī al-Dunyā, *Kitāb al-Marad wal-Kaffārāt,* ed. A.W. al-Nadwī, *al-Dār al-Salfiyyah*, Bombay, 1991.

Elgood, C., *A Medical History of Persia,* University Press, Cambridge, 1951.

El-Fandy, M.G., *Islam and Science,* 1, Cairo, 1986.

Encyclopaedia of Islam, EI^1, EI^2.

Faris, N.A., *The Book of Knowledge being a translation with notes of The Kitāb al-'Ilm of al-Ghazzali's Iḥya' 'Ulūm al-Dīn,* Sh. Muhammad Ashraf, Lahore, 1970.

Fayzee, A.A.A., *Outlines of Muhammadan Law*, third edition, Oxford University Press, Oxford, 1964.

Ghanimah, M.A.R., *Ta'rīkh al-Jāmi'āt al-Islāmiyyat al-Kubrā, Idārai-Ṭaba'at al-Maghra biyyah*, Tatwan, 1953.

Ghaznawi, K., *Ṭibb-i-Nabawī Awr Jadīd Science,* (Urdu) al-Faysal, Lahore, 1988.

Al-Ghazzali, *Iḥya' 'Ulum al-Dīn, The Book of Knowledge,* Sh. Muhammad Ashraf, Lahore, 1970.

Gibb, H.A.R., *Whither Islam*, London, 1932.

Bibliography

- , *Arabic Literature,* Oxford, 1962.

Hamarneh, S., "Development of Hospitals in Islam", in *Health Sciences in Early Islam,* Noor Health Foundation and Zahra Publications, Texas, 1983.

Hayes, J.R., (Ed.), *The Genius of Arab Civilization Source of Renaissance,* Phaidon, Oxford, 1976.

Hayward, G., *The Arts of Islam,* The Arts Council of Great Britain, 1976.

H.R.H. Prince of Wales, Islam and the West, Oxford Center for Islamic Studies, Oxford, 1993.

Ibn Hisham, *Das Leben Muhammad Nach Muhammad ibn Ishaq,*ed.: F. Wustenfeld, 1959.

Hitti, P. K., *History of the Arabs,* London, 1968.

Hussein, Suad, 'Rufida al-Asalmia- First Nurse in Islam', In: Papers Presented to the First International Conference on Islamic Medicine, El-Sayyad, I. (Ed.), International Organization of Islamic Medicine, Kuwait, 1981.

Al-Isfahani, *Ḥilyat al-Awliyā' wa Ṭabaqāt al-Aṣfiyā,* Cairo, 1351 A.H.

Ibn Jubayr, *Riḥlāt ibn Jubayr,* Gibb Memorial Series , Leiden, 1949.

Khalidi, T., *Arab Historical Thought in the Classical Age,* Cambridge University Press, Cambridge, 1994.

Khan, M., *History of Muslim Education,* (1751-1854 A.D.), Academy of Educational Research, Karachi, 1973.

Lane, E.W. *Arabic - English Lexicon,* The Islamic Text Society, Cambridge, 1984

Levy, M., Medical Ethics of Medieval Islam with Special Reference to Al-Ruḥawīs, "Practical Ethics of the Physicians", *The American Philosophical Society,* Vol. 57 part 3, pp. 1-99, 1967.

Lewis, B., *The Middle East: 2000 years of History from the Rise of Christianity to the Present Day,* London, Weidenfeld & Nicolson, 1995.

Ibn Mājah, *Sunan.*

Makdisi, G., *The Rise of Colleges: Institutions of Learning in Islam and the West,* Edinburgh University Press, Edinburgh, 1981.

-, *The Rise of Humanism in Classical Islam and Christian west,* Edingburgh University Press, 1990.

Mālik, *al-Muwaṭṭa.*

al-Marghīnānī, Burhān al-Dīn, *al-Hidāyah,* Karachi, vol. ii.

al-Maqrīzī, *Mawā'iz al-I'tibār bi Dhikr al-Khiṭaṭ wal Āthār,* , Cairo, 1908.

Mayerhofmax, *Von Alexandien nach Baghdad,* Trans. Badwi A.R. *al Turath al-Yunani Hadarat al-Islamiyah,* Beirut, n.d.

Mushtaq, Q. and Tan A.L., *Mathematics: The Islamic Legacy,* Noor Publishing House, Delhi, 1983.

Muslim, *al-Jāmi' al-Ṣaḥīḥ.*

Ibn Nadīm, *al-Fihrist,* Liepzig, 1871.

al-Nadwī, A.W. (Ed.), Ibn Abī al-Dunyā, *Kitāb al-Marad wal-Kaffārāt,* Bombay, 1991.

Nadvi S.S., *The Arab Navigation,* Sh. Muhammad Ashraf, Lahore, 1966.

Naqui, S.H.Z., 'Islam and Development of Science', *Nigerian Journal of Islam,* vol. i p. 5, 1971-1972.

al-Nasā'ī, *Sunan*

al-Nasimī, M.N., *al-Ṭibb al-Nabawī wal 'Ilm al-Ḥadīth, Mu'assisah al-Risālah,* Beirut, 1987.

Nasr, S.H., *An Introduction to Islamic Cosmological Doctrines,* Haward University Press, Cambridge, 1964.

Nasr, S.H., *Islamic Science An Illustrated Study,* World of Islam Festival Publishing Company Ltd., London, 1976.

Nasr, S.H., *Science and Civilization in Islam,* Cambridge (U.S.A.), 1968.

al-Qiftī, *Ikhbār al-'Ulamā' bi Akhbār al-Ḥukamā',* Egypt, 1326 A.H..

al-Sarakhsī, *al-Mabsūṭ,* Cairo, vol. xii, 1324 A.H.

Sarton, G., *A Guide to the History of Science,* The Ronald Press, New York, 1952.

Sezgin, F., *Ta'rīkh Ulūm mayn Tahzeeb-i-Islāmī kā Maqām* (Urdu), Translated by K. Ridwī, *Idārah Taḥqīqah Islāmī,* 1994.

al-Sibā'ī,M., *Min Rawā'i Haḍāratinā al-Islāmiyyah,* Beirut, 1977.

as-Suyūti, J.A.R., *As Suyūti's Medicine of the Prophet,* Ta-Ha Publishers Ltd, London,1994.

Bibliography

Surty, M.I.H.I., *Islam: The Qur'anic Overview*, QAF Qur'anic Arabic Foundation, Birmingham, 1995.

-, *Halal Food in the Light of the Qur'an and Sunnah*, QAF, Birmingham 1995.

al-Ṭabarī, Muḥammad bin Jarīr, *Annales*, ed. De Goeje, Brill, 1879-1901.

Ibn Taghrī Birdī, *al-Nujūm al-Zāhirah fī Mulūk Miṣr wal Qāhirah,* T.G.J. Juynboll, (Ed.), Leiden, 1855.

Rahman, Tanzil-ur-, *A Code of Muslim Personal Law*, Islamic Publishers, Karachi, vol. ii, 1980.

Rogers, M., *The Making of the Past: The Spread of Islam,* Oxford, Elsevier Phaidon, 1976.

al-Tirmidhī, *al-Jāmi' al-Ṣaḥīḥ*.

Ibn Abī Usaybī'ah Abū Dāwūd Sulaymān bin Hassan, *Ṭabaqāt al-Aṭibbā' wal Hukamā',* Egypt, 1955.

Wāstī N.A. A., *Ṭibb al-'Arab,* Translation of E.G. Brown, *Arabian Medicine,* Lahore, 1969.

Wensinck A.J., *Concordance et Indices de la Tradition Musulmane,* E. J. Brill, Leiden, 1936.

Abū Yūsuf, *Kitāb al-Kharāj*, Egypt, 2nd edition, 1933.

Zaydān, J., *Ta'rīkh al-Tamaddun al-Islāmī,* beirut, n. d.

Towards Understanding

Qur'ānic Arabic

A Manual Teaching Arabic Through the Qur'ān

(Elementary)

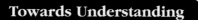

Muhammad Ibrahim H I Surty

QAF Qur'ānic Arabic Foundation

Islam: The Qur'ānic Overview

by Dr Muhammad Ibrahim H I Surty

•

This work provides the principal teachings, concepts, institutions and thoughts of the Qur'ān in less than **an hour**.

•

Contains over 650 references to the Qur'ān and serves as a guide book for both students and teachers.

•

33 Qur'ānic aspects are presented in points form.

•

Presents the House of Islam and its comprehensive teachings in points form, covering all aspects of human life.

•

Extremely useful for both Muslims and non-Muslims.

•

32 pp Special offer of £1.00 + postage.

QAF: Qur'ānic Arabic Foundation

QAF 552B Coventry Road, Small Heath , Birmingham B10 0UN, England, UK
Telephone 021 771 1894 Facsimile 021 476 8428

HALAL FOOD

in the light of the

Qur'ān and Sunnah

(An overview)

by Muhammad Ibrahim H.I. Surty

• This monograph gives reasons for the question Why Halal Food?

• Presents Qur'ānic dietetic legislations based on spiritual grounds and physical grounds.

• Qur'ānic legislations are made clear with *aḥādīth* of the Prophet (Peace be upon him)

Price: 75p. only + postage

QAF: Qur'anic Arabic Foundation
QAF 552B Coventry Road, Small Heath , Birmingham B10 0UN, England, UK
Telephone 0121 771 1894 Facsimile 0121 476 8428

About the Author

Dr Muhammad Ibrahim H. I Surty, (b.1941) B.A (Hons.) M.A.(Bom) Ph.D, (London).

Dr Surty served for several years the University of Sokoto as Reader and Head of the Department of Islamic Studies. He is a Senior Lecturer at CSIC, University of Birmingham and Chairman of the QAF Trust.

His works include *Adab al-Qāḍī* two vols • *The Qur'ān and al-Shirk* • *A Course in ʿIlm al-Tajwīd: the Science of Reciting the Qur'ān*• *Islam: The Qur'ānic Overview* •*The Qur'ānic Concept of God* •*Muslims' Contribution to the Development of Hospitals* •*Halal Food in the Light of the Qur'ān and Sunnah* •*Qur'ānic Arabic : A Manual Teaching Arabic Through the Qur'ān.* He has contributed several articles on different Islamic themes in the literary journals.